M364
UNDERGRADUATE COMPUTING

Fundamentals of interaction design

Design

Block 3

This publication forms part of an Open University course M364 *Fundamentals of interaction design*. Details of this and other Open University courses can be obtained from the Customer Contact Centre, The Open University, Milton Keynes, MK7 6AA, United Kingdom: tel. +44 (0)1908 653231, email general-enquiries@open.ac.uk

Alternatively, you may visit the Open University website at **www.open.ac.uk** where you can learn more about the wide range of courses and packs offered at all levels by The Open University.

To purchase a selection of Open University course materials visit the webshop at **www.ouw.co.uk**, or contact Open University Worldwide, Michael Young Building, Walton Hall, Milton Keynes MK7 6AA,
United Kingdom for a brochure. tel. +44 (0)1908 858785; fax +44 (0)1908 858787; email ouwenq@open.ac.uk

The Open University
Walton Hall, Milton Keynes
MK7 6AA

First published 2005

Edited and designed by The Open University.

Typeset by The Open University.

Printed and bound in the United Kingdom by Thanet Press Ltd, Margate.

ISBN 0 7492 0276 9

1.1

Block 3
Design

CONTENTS

M364 COURSE TEAM

Helen Sharp, Chair and Author

Judith Segal, Author

Debbie Stone, Author

Mark Woodroffe, Author

Mary King, Course Manager

Persefoni Stylianoudaki, Course Manager

Media development staff

John O'Dwyer, Media Project Manager

Andrew Seddon, Media Project Manager

Garry Hammond, Editor

Andrew Whitehead, Designer

Phillip Howe, Compositor

Vicky Eves, Graphic Artist

Mark Mulrooney, Software Developer

External assessor

Ann Blandford, University College London

Critical readers

Sandra Cairncross, Napier University

Gloria Chew

Ian Graydon

John Morris

Thanks are due to the Desktop Publishing Unit of the Faculty of Mathematics and Computing.

Introduction to Block 3

Block introduction

In Block 2, you will have learned about identifying needs and establishing the requirements for an interactive product. At the end of Block 2 Unit 2, the author suggested that the following would inform the design of the interactive product:

▶ an understanding of user requirements (characteristics), as represented perhaps by a set of personas

▶ a set of scenarios of users' existing behaviour, and their envisioned behaviour when interacting with the product

▶ a set of use cases of users' interactions with the envisioned product (these may be derived from the scenarios)

▶ a set of essential use cases describing user intentions and system responsibilities (these may be derived from use cases)

▶ (possibly) an analysis of a small task into subtasks

▶ a set of requirements described, perhaps, using a Volere shell. These might be functional or non-functional, the latter being informed by the personas and the scenarios.

In addition, the interaction designer should be armed with a set of specific usability and user experience goals.

In this block we will focus on how to take this set of information and produce an appropriate design. In terms of the simple interaction design model you met in Block 1, Block 3 focuses on two of the activities: '(Re)Design' and 'Build an interactive version' (see figure). Building an interactive version can involve prototyping and construction.

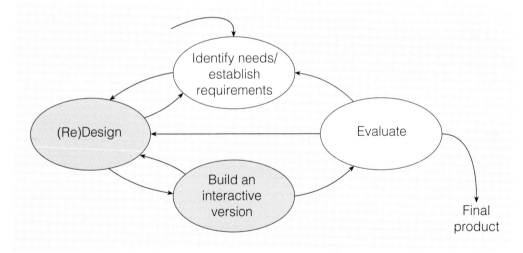

Design is not an easy skill to teach as it has many different facets, and is viewed differently by different disciplines. As an example, consider the following account, summarised from Dorst (2003, p. 14):

The same puzzle was given to two sets of students: one group studying mathematics, and one group studying architecture. The mathematicians started by analysing the problem, and once they had understood it, they tried to solve it. All the mathematicians solved the problem fairly quickly. The architects, on the other hand, began by laying out possible solutions and then trying to improve them. Apparently the architects were used to tackling problems that did not lend themselves to analysis. Instead they would suggest highly likely solutions and then analyse those, evaluate them and improve them. The mathematicians focused on the problem and analysed that, while the architects focused on possible solutions and analysed those.

This difference of approach is useful when considering interaction design. In fact, the approach taken by this course involves a combination of both of the strategies above: first analyse the problem, then suggest likely solutions and analyse, evaluate and improve them. The iterative nature of the process also means that the activities are intertwined; for example, in practice you're likely to be thinking of possible conceptual models while undertaking the requirements activity. In this case, you have jumped to a solution which you then would evaluate and improve.

You may find it helpful to remember these two different approaches to design while studying this block.

The block contains the following four units.

Unit 1: Understanding and conceptualising interaction

This unit explores ways in which the design process can proceed without concentrating on the detailed design level. In particular, we discuss the importance of investigating the problem space of a product, different conceptual models that may help envision the new product, and we give initial consideration to how the design process might move forward from conceptual design to physical design. Three key concepts explored in this unit are: conceptual models, interface metaphors, and interaction paradigms.

At the end of this unit you will not be expected to develop your own conceptual model, but you will be able to understand what a conceptual model is and to recognise different types. Unit 4 will show you how to develop a conceptual model.

Unit 2: Choosing interaction devices

Most PCs have a keyboard and a mouse as input devices, and a screen and a printer as output devices. Loudspeakers may also be used for sound output, and a joystick or steering wheel may be used for input, particularly if games are being played on the computer. However, there are many different types of input and output devices available, and choosing appropriate devices will help to ensure that usability and user experience goals are met. This unit introduces different kinds of interaction devices and offers some guidance to help choose between alternatives for a particular interactive product.

Unit 3: Understanding users

In this unit we will look at what can be learned from the work of cognitive science that can be helpful in designing interactive products for people. Understanding some of the characteristics and limitations of the human mind will help you to see why some designs work well and others fail miserably. It will also help you to understand and apply suitable design guidelines. The unit includes the following topics: cognitive processes, implications for interaction design of these processes, mental models, information processing and external cognition.

Although Unit 3 appears to be quite short, it can take some time to fully understand the concepts it contains. To help you understand them better, and to relate them to your own experiences, there is an 'Experience Record Sheet' in the appendix. I suggest that you copy this and have it with you while you are studying this unit so that you can record examples of the concepts that you meet during your everyday activities.

Unit 4: Design, prototyping and construction

Unit 4 pulls together much of the material introduced in the previous three units, and provides some practical guidance on how to produce the first design for the interactive product under development. Specifically, this unit teaches you about prototyping: the reasons for prototyping, and issues concerned with the different kinds of prototyping.

It also teaches you how to produce three kinds of low-fidelity prototype: a storyboard which helps explore the environment of the product, a card-based prototype which represents the task flow and high-level design for the product, and interface sketches which require more details about the product.

Block learning outcomes

This block contains a combination of theory and practical application.

For the complete list of learning outcomes for the course, see the *Course Guide*.

In particular, this block contributes to the following course learning outcomes:

Knowledge and understanding

KU1: Explain why it is important to design interactive products that are usable.

KU2: Define key terms used in interaction design.

KU5: Explain the importance of iteration, evaluation and prototyping in interaction design.

KU6: Discuss theoretical or empirical evidence supporting a list of interaction design principles.

KU7: Discuss accessibility issues for interactive products.

Cognitive skills

CS1: Evaluate an interactive product using suitable techniques.

CS4: Produce a low-fidelity prototype for an interactive product based upon a simple list of interaction design principles.

Key skills

KS1: Construct and convey an argument from a variety of sources to persuade a non-specialist audience of the importance of user-centred design when designing interactive products.

KS2: Communicate effectively to peers and specialists about requirements, design and evaluation activities relating to interactive products.

Specific outcomes of this block

LO1: Explain what is meant by the problem space for an intended product.

LO2: Define what a conceptual model is, and say what it is not.

LO3: Provide and recognise examples of two different kinds of conceptual model: activity-based and object-based.

LO4: Discuss the pros and cons of using interface metaphors as conceptual models.

LO5: Describe different interaction paradigms and give examples of each.

LO6: Outline the relationship between conceptual design and physical design.

LO7: Describe a variety of interaction devices.

LO8: Explain the significance of choosing the right interaction device.

LO9: Describe the difference between direct and indirect pointing devices and give examples of each.

LO10: Describe the difference between continuous and discrete interaction devices, and give examples of each.

LO11: Choose suitable interaction devices for a simple interactive product.

LO12: Explain what cognition is and why it is important for interaction design.

LO13: Describe the cognitive processes of attention, perception and recognition, memory, learning, reading, speaking and listening, and problem-solving, planning, reasoning and decision-making.

LO14: Discuss, justify and apply a set of design implications that arise from the cognitive processes in LO13.

LO15: Explain what a mental model is and its significance to interaction design.

LO16: Define information processing and external cognition as frameworks for cognition.

LO17: Describe the user's model, design model and system image, and the relationships between them.

LO18: Elicit a mental model and be able to understand what it means.

LO19: Describe prototyping and different types of prototyping activities.

LO20: Explain the benefits of paper-based prototyping.

LO21: Develop and expand a conceptual model for an interactive product.

LO22: Develop three kinds of low-fidelity prototype for an interactive product: a storyboard, a card-based prototype, and a detailed interface sketch.

LO23: Apply a suitable set of design principles and rules for the design of an interactive product.

LO24: Design an appropriate icon for use in a low-fidelity prototype.

Unit 1: Understanding and conceptualising interaction

CONTENTS

Introduction to Unit 1

Once a set of stable requirements has emerged, the next step in the interaction design process is to produce a design of the product. However, it can be difficult to know where to start. It is easiest to start at the physical level, thinking of concrete widgets, colours, shapes and so on, but if we do this then key usability goals may be overlooked. This unit explores ways in which the design process can proceed without concentrating at the detailed design level. In particular, we will discuss the importance of investigating the problem space of a product and different conceptual models that may help envision the new product. We will also give initial consideration to how the design process might move forward from conceptual design to physical design.

Three key concepts that are explored in this unit are:

1 *Conceptual models.* In this unit, I describe what a conceptual model needs to capture – what the proposed system should do, how it should behave and what it should look like – and the two main kinds of conceptual model – those based on activities and those based on objects.

2 *Interface metaphors.* In this unit we will explore metaphors and their use in design. One of the earliest metaphors employed in software design was the spreadsheet. The electronic version is based on its paper predecessor, thus drawing on the users' familiarity with an existing paper-based entity to help them learn the new system. The electronic version, however, has considerably more functionality as the designers exploited the electronic medium.

3 *Interaction paradigms.* These represent different ways of thinking about an interaction, for example considering mobile technology instead of focusing on one user and their personal computer. In this unit, we will consider different kinds of interaction paradigm that are available.

In Unit 4 of this block, I will show how conceptual models, interface metaphors and interaction paradigms can be used to create a prototype of the product under development.

This unit introduces some new and fairly difficult concepts. Although you may be able to read through the material in less time than the Study Calendar suggests, I recommend that you reflect on what you've learned, and re-visit the Set Book after going through the extension material here.

Conceptual models were introduced in Block 1 Unit 4, as being the focus of conceptual design.

Interface metaphors were introduced in Block 1 Unit 4.

What you need to study this unit

You will need the following course components:

▶ this book

▶ the book *Interaction Design* by Preece, Rogers and Sharp (from here on this is referred to as the Set Book)

▶ the course DVD.

You will need your computer for some of the activities.

How to study this unit

This unit is based around Chapter 2 of the Set Book.

STUDY NOTE

I suggest that you start by reading the whole of Chapter 2, including the boxes, and complete the activities as you read, making notes or highlighting key sections. You do not need to complete the Assignment on page 68. However, you should read through the summary and key points of the chapter listed on pages 68–69 and check that you understand them.

Then study the additional material, readings, activities and review questions that follow in this book. These are organised in a similar way to Chapter 2 of the Set Book and are designed to both deepen and broaden your understanding of interaction design. Completing the activities will often require you to re-read sections of the Set Book, so they should help consolidate your understanding and mean you remember more when you come to revising.

1 Understanding the problem space

1.1 Review of the Set Book reading

> ### STUDY NOTE
>
> This section complements and extends Sections 2.1 and 2.2 in the Set Book. If you have not already read these sections of the Set Book, then I suggest that you do so before reading any further.

Sections 2.1 and 2.2 explain why it is not appropriate to start thinking about design at the physical level, however attractive this may seem. Instead, this unit advocates starting the design process by reflecting on what you intend to create, thinking through how it will support people in their everyday or working lives, considering whether it will support people in the way you intend and justifying why you want to create it. In particular, there will be a set of assumptions underlying this intention, relating to user needs, usability goals and user experience goals. Uncovering and challenging these assumptions will give you a better understanding of what you are trying to achieve, and will refine the existing goals and requirements.

In the Set Book, this process is expressed as 'understanding the problem space' of the intended product. The **problem space** for a particular product is defined as the range of possible conceptual models for the product, together with their rationales, i.e. their advantages, disadvantages, implications and justifications. You do not need to develop a range of conceptual models to any level of detail in order to do this, and the Set Book suggests a set of questions to ask that will help uncover the relevant assumptions.

Review Question 1

Why is it inappropriate to start designing at the physical level?

Review Question 2

What activities are central to working out the problem space for a product?

Review Question 3

Write down three sets of questions that you can ask of a situation that will help you to start exploring the problem space.

Review Question 4

What approaches can you use to explore the problem space of a product?

The following activity will give you some practice in exploring assumptions for a particular product.

ACTIVITY 1

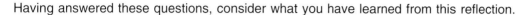

Imagine that you have come up with the idea of developing the first automatic bread-making machine intended for use in the home. Assume that there are no bread-making machines currently available – you just know that making bread can be a messy and time-consuming activity, yet eating freshly-made bread is wonderful. Use the questions listed on page 38 of the Set Book to articulate the assumptions and claims about why the product is a good idea.

Having answered these questions, consider what you have learned from this reflection.

COMMENT

You may have come up with slightly different answers to mine, depending on your perspective of bread-making. To answer these questions for a product you were developing, you would investigate the issues in more depth.

Are there problems with an existing product? There are no existing products, but the current process of making bread is messy and time-consuming, and not everyone is skilled in bread-making.

Why do you think there are problems? I know there are problems because I've made bread in the past.

Why do you think your proposed ideas might be useful? From my own experience, I think having a simple, mess-free, automatic way to make bread is very appealing. However, I would have to do some more investigation in order to gauge the potential popularity of my idea.

How do you envision people integrating your proposed design with how they currently do things in their everyday or working lives? I would want to design the bread-maker to be automatic with very little intervention required from the beginning to the end of the process. Apart from supplying the ingredients, I would not want to be involved in the process. It could therefore be working overnight, or while I'm out doing other things. There may be a balance to be struck here between achieving low intervention and having a product that can make several different types of bread. Where to place the emphasis will be influenced by the product's goals.

How will your proposed design support people in their activities? In what way does it address an identified problem or extend current ways of doing things? Will it really help? This product will support people in their everyday lives by providing a simple way to produce fresh bread. For some people this may mean being able to bake their own bread for the first time.

Having been through this list of questions, I would conclude that the product is worth investigating further. I am clear about the problem that it is intended to solve, I can see how the product might fit into a person's everyday and working life, and that it will support them. My next step would be to consult potential users to confirm my views. Having done so, I would return to these questions and see if any of the answers had changed.

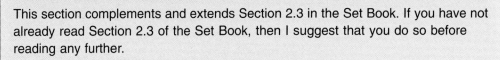

2 Conceptual models

2.1 Review of the Set Book reading

Section 2.3 is a long section that focuses on describing conceptual models and explaining some different kinds of conceptual model. At the end of this section you should be able to recognise different types of conceptual model, and describe the information that a conceptual model should convey. At this point, you will not be expected to be able to develop your own conceptual model.

According to the Set Book, page 40, a **conceptual model** is:

> a description of the proposed system in terms of a set of integrated ideas and concepts about
>
> ▶ what it should do,
>
> ▶ how it should behave and
>
> ▶ what it should look like,
>
> that will be understandable by the users in the manner intended.

This clearly identifies three aspects of a conceptual model, but a conceptual model is an abstract view of the product and so none of these aspects will be worked out in detail. For example, identifying 'what it should look like' does not mean that the conceptual model includes detailed drawings of the layout, button designs, choice of colours, etc. However, it does mean that alternative styles have been considered and that, for example, the system will be similar to a desk diary rather than a wall calendar. Conceptual models come in many different styles, and it is not possible to state prescriptively what a conceptual model is, but it should capture each of these three aspects of the design. One of the key characteristics of a conceptual model is that it considers what is needed rather than the detail of how it should be achieved.

Section 2.3 in the Set Book describes two main kinds of conceptual model: those based on activities and those based on objects. The most common activities forming the basis of the former are: instructing, conversing, manipulating and navigating, and exploring and browsing. You may have felt that these are very tightly linked with the details of the interface design for the product, which is not the focus of conceptual design; however these different forms of activity capture some very different kinds of interaction.

This can be illustrated by considering how the interaction would change if the type of activity was different. For example, consider how you would interact with a vending machine if a navigating and exploring style were adopted, or how you would interact with a computer game if instructing was the only style of interaction. Indeed, the early forms of adventure games were developed before GUI interfaces or direct manipulation were commonly available, and they relied solely on command-based instruction, which made the user experience very different from the equivalent games available today (see Box 1). In this case, the task required a manipulating and navigating type of interaction, but the technology limited the possibilities. Although this is an extreme example, the same effect could be achieved if a designer chooses the wrong kind of conceptual model for a task.

Box 1: Adventure games played from a command-line interface

The first adventure game, Zork, was published in 1981. The game was completely text (character) based. The user would type in a question or an instruction, press enter, and the system would respond with a textual description of the result of this action followed by a further prompt. For example in the transcript below the user asks the system to 'examine window' (note that this represents a physical window, not an element of a computer interface), and is told that the window is 'slightly ajar, but not enough to allow entry'. The user then decides to 'open window', and so on.

Much of the game revolved around finding items, such as the glass bottle with water in it mentioned below, and performing suitable actions with the items, such as drinking the water or throwing it at a fire-eating dragon. Part of the excitement is the result of not knowing when or if an item will be of use to you (how much can you carry?), and not having a map of the environment within which you are playing.

This is an example where the technology limits the kind of conceptual model for interaction that is possible. The kind of task is manipulating and navigating, yet the technology forces more of an 'instructing' kind of interaction.

```
 Kitchen                                    Score: 10        Moves: 11

>e
Behind House
You are behind the white house. A path leads into the forest to the east. In
one corner of the house there is a small window which is slightly ajar.

>examine window
The window is slightly ajar, but not enough to allow entry.

>open window
With great effort, you open the window far enough to allow entry.

>enter
Kitchen
You are in the kitchen of the white house. A table seems to have been used
recently for the preparation of food. A passage leads to the west and a dark
staircase can be seen leading upward. A dark chimney leads down and to the
east is a small window which is open.
On the table is an elongated brown sack, smelling of hot peppers.
A bottle is sitting on the table.
The glass bottle contains:
   A quantity of water

>
```

Transcript from the adventure game, Zork

Conceptual models based on objects can provide a more holistic description of the intended product, as an object can embody functionality, behaviour and appearance. This idea is linked to interface metaphors (discussed below) but use of a metaphor revolves around there being a familiar entity with which to compare the new system or product; a conceptual model based on objects does not rely on other familiar experience. For example, in a system to support mortgage applications, the interaction may be structured around a mortgage application entity whether or not the users are expected to be familiar with mortgage applications.

Choosing which of these two types of conceptual model is most appropriate depends on the tasks the user will be performing (and hence relies upon information gleaned through the requirements activity). However, things are not always very clear-cut, and the section ends with the observation that it is often appropriate to include different kinds of conceptual model within one product because the tasks being accomplished vary throughout the functions of the product.

We will discuss Box 2.3 of the Set Book in Unit 3, Section 3.

Box 2.3 on page 54 of the Set Book contains some important ideas regarding the need for the conceptual model to be understandable by users. Don Norman suggested that, in an ideal world, the three key models in interaction design (the design model, the user's model and the system image) should map onto each other.

Review Question 5

The definition of conceptual model given in this section refers to three aspects of the intended product that should be described in the product's conceptual model. What are these three aspects?

Review Question 6

What are the two main kinds of conceptual model?

Section 2.3 in the Set Book introduces the terms interaction mode and interaction style. The interaction mode for a particular product refers to whether the conceptual model is object-based or activity-based. The interaction style chosen is dependent on the appropriate mode, but is more concerned with detailed physical level design and so is not considered in any detail during conceptual design.

Understanding and developing conceptual models is a complex area of interaction design, and so in the following sections I provide some further discussion and activities to help you assimilate these ideas. First of all, I will indicate how you might go about developing a conceptual model. This is just to give you a flavour of an approach, and I will consider developing conceptual models further in Unit 4. Then I consider what a conceptual model is, and dispel some misunderstandings by considering also what it is not. The section ends with a computer activity in which you can experience different forms of one important element of the conceptual model for a website: the navigation structure.

2.2 An initial consideration of how to develop a conceptual model

Developing your own conceptual model is not an objective of this unit, however you may at this point be wondering how the model is identified and how it is captured. You may want to know in detail what a conceptual model looks like. There is no straightforward answer to this question, but probably the simplest way to develop a conceptual model is to say that the new product will be 'like' some other product or system. Having established what it will be like, the task then involves detailing specifically how the new product will differ from the existing one.

Remember that Block 1 discussed the role that previous designs can have in developing new ones.

For example, in a vehicle navigation system designed to provide drivers with access to map and route information (Marcus, 2000), it was decided that the product should appear to be an extension of existing vehicle dashboard controls. This decision was based on user research. Once this was established as the main concept, then elements of how the system should behave and what it should look like followed automatically.

It is still important to identify the right kind of product which the new development will be like, and to make sound decisions about how it will differ. The sources on which to base your decisions, and the kinds of technique for capturing the model include: the output of the requirements activity (e.g. may be captured in a set of Volere shells), existing products or systems in the same or similar market, usability goals, and user experience goals.

You met Volere shells for capturing requirements in Block 2 Unit 2.

There are a lot of issues to juggle, which is why an iterative approach is most appropriate.

We will return to developing conceptual models in Unit 4.

2.3 What a conceptual model is, and what it is not

I have stated above that a conceptual model should capture three aspects of an intended product: what the product should do, how it should behave and what it should look like. However it is difficult to grasp the essentials of a conceptual model and what it means to develop one, so in this section we present an alternative but complementary way of thinking about conceptual models which is based on an article by Johnson and Henderson (2002).

In their article, Johnson and Henderson describe a conceptual model as 'an idealized view of how the system works – the model designers hope users will internalize'. In the following extract, they go on to describe conceptual models in more detail and provide some concrete examples. Note that they refer to 'systems' but their comments apply equally to all interactive products.

A conceptual model is a high-level description of how a system is organized and operates. It specifies and describes:

▶ The major design metaphors and analogies employed in the design, if any.

▶ The concepts the system exposes to users, including the task-domain data-objects users create and manipulate, their attributes, and the operations that can be performed on them.

▶ The relationships between these concepts.

▶ The mappings between the concepts and the task-domain the system is designed to support.

A task-domain data-object is an item from the product's application domain that the users may want to store or access information about, e.g. the library catalogue items listed below.

For example, suppose you are designing an online library catalogue. The conceptual model might include:

▶ Metaphors and analogies: e.g. the information is organized as in a physical card-catalogue.

▶ Concepts: e.g. item (with attributes: title, ISBN, status, with actions: check-out, check-in, reserve), subtypes of item (e.g. book, periodical issue, LP, video), periodical volume, user account (with attributes: name, items checked out), librarian.

▶ Relationships: e.g. a book is one type of item, periodical volumes contain issues.

▶ Mappings: e.g. each item in the system corresponds to a physical item in the library.

Source: Johnson and Henderson (2002)

They go on to say that a conceptual model should be as simple as possible while still supporting the required functionality, and that there should be a clear mapping between the system and the task domain being supported. This is to help the users understand the system so that their model of it is as accurate as possible.

ACTIVITY 2

We will discuss metaphors in the next section, so here I will ask you to focus on the other three elements described by Johnson and Henderson: concepts exposed to users, relationships between concepts, and mappings between concepts and task-domain.

Compare their view of a conceptual model with the three aspects of a conceptual model described in the Set Book: what it should do, how it should behave, and what it should look like.

COMMENT

I consider each of the elements and discuss their similarity with the Set Book view below.

▶ *The concepts the system exposes to users, including the task-domain data-objects users create and manipulate, their attributes, and the operations that can be performed on them.* This is a more detailed description of what the product will do, how it will behave, and what it will look like, which focuses on task-domain objects and the mapping between these and concepts within the interactive product.

▶ *The relationships between these concepts.* The relationship is linked to how the product will behave and what it will be able to do.

▶ *The mappings between the concepts and the task-domain the system is designed to support.* This is both what it will do and how it will behave, as the user will expect concepts in the product to behave and appear similar to the corresponding concept in the task-domain.

They also say what a conceptual model is not:

The conceptual model of an interactive system is *not the user interface*. It is not about how the software looks or feels. ... It describes only what people can do with the system and what concepts they need to understand to operate it. ... The conceptual model is *not the user's mental model* of the system ... Conceptual models are more usefully thought of as a design-tool – a way for designers to straighten out their thinking before they start laying out widgets ... The conceptual models are *not use cases* ... Finally a conceptual model is *not an implementation architecture* ... .

It is worth expanding on these comments to explain why the conceptual model is none of these things. The conceptual model is *not* the user interface because the interface is only one implementation of a conceptual model, and there will be many possible implementations. Designing the interface requires a lot of detailed decision-making regarding screen layout, use of colour, size and positioning of buttons or menus, etc. The conceptual model ignores these detailed design issues and deliberately forces the designer to think more abstractly. A **mental model** is a mental construct within the head of the user which consists of knowledge of how to use something and knowledge of how it works. The conceptual model is *not* the users' mental model of the system, therefore, since the former is generated through the design process, while the latter evolves with use of the system. One of the aims of design is to help users develop a mental model of the system that matches the designer's own model.

We discuss users' mental models in Unit 3 of this block.

ACTIVITY 3

Why is a conceptual model not a set of use cases?

COMMENT

Use cases were introduced in Block 2. They are a good way of capturing task description. As with the interface, however, use cases are expressed at a level of detail that is too low for a conceptual model, and represent one possible interaction style, but not the only one. In addition, use cases focus at the task level, while a conceptual model is concerned with the system as a whole.

Finally, the focus of an implementation architecture is on technology and instantiation issues rather than on understanding the users' interaction with the system. An implementation architecture is also unlikely to be understandable by most users.

ACTIVITY

Computer Activity 1: Navigational structure

This activity will take approximately one hour

One important element of the conceptual model for a website is the kind of navigation it uses. This characterises the possible interactions between the user and the website, and influences the way the site will behave, the way it will look and what it will be able to do.

In this activity, on the course DVD, you will experience different types of navigation aids and how these can affect interaction.

Note that the usability evaluation teaching you will meet through this activity does *not* form part of the study text for M364, and you will not be assessed on it.

3 | Interface metaphors

3.1 | Review of the Set Book reading

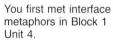

You first met interface metaphors in Block 1 Unit 4.

This section expands on the idea of an **interface metaphor**, i.e. an entity which will be familiar to the intended users, and will form the basis of the design of an interaction. Metaphors are commonly employed in teaching and training environments, and in everyday conversation, to communicate about new or unfamiliar ideas and concepts, using more familiar and better understood concepts. Metaphors are popular because they can communicate a lot of information, based on experience, relatively quickly. For example, saying that atoms are structured like a solar system, with a nucleus as the 'sun' and electrons as the 'planets', communicates far more quickly the basic structure of an atom than trying to explain it from scratch. In a similar way, using a familiar entity from the users' domain can communicate a lot to the users and can help them to understand how a system works.

A metaphor may be used in interaction design in two different ways: the metaphor may become part of the final system and will help users to understand the system; or the metaphor may be used as a vehicle for the designer to explore and communicate ideas to other designers. For example, the Set Book (Box 2.2 on page 53) describes the development of the Star system and the use of an office metaphor. This metaphor was built into the final system and was intended to simplify and clarify interaction with the users. The Star developers considered a variety of metaphors before choosing this one. Designers often draw on a wide variety of metaphors when developing a conceptual model, and although they may not make their way into the final system in any recognisable form, they can help with the thinking process that results in the final conceptual model.

The use of metaphors is controversial, and although on balance they are generally seen as beneficial, the designer must be clear about which aspects of a metaphor are relevant for the system under development.

Review Question 7

What is the main benefit of using an interface metaphor?

Review Question 8

Summarise the arguments against using interface metaphors.

Review Question 9

Which aspects of the conceptual model might be informed by the choice of interface metaphor?

Using appropriate metaphors can cause problems, as discussed in Review Question 8, but inappropriate metaphors that are built into the user interface can be downright confusing and misleading. The next section illustrates this with some examples.

We will look at how to choose appropriate metaphors in Unit 4 of this block.

3.2 Metaphors can be harmful

There are several metaphors in common use within software applications, most of which are accepted as being helpful, and all of which have been modified to suit the electronic environment. Examples include the shopping basket metaphor on ecommerce sites, the desktop metaphor for personal computers, cut-and-paste metaphors in word processors, and so on.

However, there are some examples where a common metaphor is misleading. For example, consider the command 'delete' used in computer systems. The action the software performs when asked to 'delete' a file is to remove the file header, i.e. the mechanism the operating system uses to identify where the file is stored. It does not wipe the file contents from the disk. If the space is not overwritten, the contents can be retrieved. This can be a problem if a disk containing (deleted) sensitive data falls into the wrong hands.

In some cases, it is unclear why a particular metaphor has been chosen, as it seems so completely inappropriate. For example, the print dialogue box shown in Figure 1 appears in the Interface Hall of Shame. It uses a video cassette recorder (VCR) metaphor for the controls. The stop and pause buttons are understandable, but what does the rewind button do? Also, where is the play button?

Figure 1   Inappropriate use of the VCR controls metaphor

In other cases, the conceptual model captured by the metaphor is appropriate in some circumstances, but not in all. The example in Figure 2 uses the 'wizard' metaphor. This metaphor is commonly used in many applications for guiding novice users, or where the task is complex or infrequently performed. When used appropriately, the wizard is ideal, but it necessarily involves taking users through a simple step-by-step process which is not appropriate for expert users or for frequently performed tasks.

eZip is a utility to create, modify and decompress Zip files. A Zip file is created by taking a number of files and compressing them, thus producing a file that contains all the original information, but takes up less storage. Zip files are particularly useful for storing or transmitting large files, as the Zipped version is a lot smaller than the original in most cases.

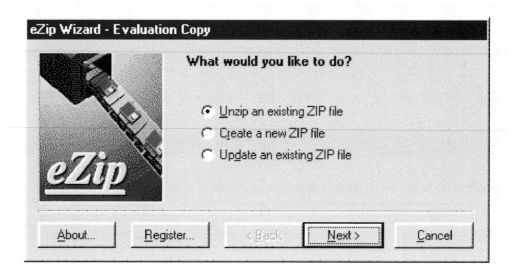

Figure 2   Example of a 'wizard' metaphor, used in the eZip utility

The problem with wizards in general, and with eZip in particular, is that they enforce a linear arrangement on the interface: the user must follow the steps the developer programmed into the application. This can be useful for the first-time or infrequent user, but can be frustrating for the experienced user. In eZip, the steps are defined as a fixed series of questions:

▶ 'What would you like to do?'

▶ 'What options do you want?'

▶ 'What name do you want to use?'

▶ etc.

The user must respond to each question before proceeding to the next step.

The first-time user may find the structure helpful, but users who frequently create or modify Zip files will find the structure unacceptable: even the relatively simple process of adding or removing a file becomes an interrogation. An alternative might be to keep the wizard metaphor for novice users but to include other metaphors for more experienced users.

Sometimes a problem with a metaphor might not be the metaphor itself but how it's been implemented. We will explore an example of this in the following activity.

ACTIVITY 4

The application explored in this activity requires a large amount of information to be entered. The designers wanted to use a simple metaphor to inform users about how much information they have entered, and how much they still have left to enter.

The metaphor chosen was a traffic light. The idea was to use the colours of a traffic light to indicate when all the information had been entered and the user could proceed.

(a) Assuming that this application is to run in an office environment, used by employed adults, consider the metaphor itself, and comment briefly on its likely suitability.

The screen below shows an implementation of this metaphor, and is taken from the Interface Hall of Shame. The process of entering the information is split across several tabs, and so the designers decided to use the traffic light metaphor for each tab. The traffic light symbols are displayed in the lower-right corner of the window to indicate the user's progress through the information entering process. Light 1 relates to the first tab, light 2 relates to the second tab, and so on. Each light can be any of three colours, with the following meanings:

Red: Not all required information has been entered.

Yellow: Some information has been entered.

Green: All required information has been entered.

Figure 3 An interface using a traffic light metaphor

(b) Identify three problems with the implementation of this metaphor.

COMMENT

(a) The answer to this question depends on the culture in which the application is to run. It is reasonable to assume that adults will be familiar with traffic lights in their own country, but there are differences in meaning for the 'amber' (yellow) light in different countries, and so the implementation needs to take this into account. Colours also have different meanings in different cultures, and so it would be necessary to check that the notion of 'green' for 'go' and 'red' for 'stop' are accepted within the culture of the user community. Assuming that these issues are sorted out, then the metaphor is likely to be suitable.

> We discussed differences in culture that need to be considered, in Block 2 Unit 1.

(b) The following three areas are listed at the Interface Hall of Shame:

Too much information. The traffic light metaphor requires the user to learn the meanings of three states, when only one is necessary. The only important indication to the user is that required information on a particular tab is missing. Thus, the interface is unnecessarily cluttered. In addition, I would add that the difference between what red and yellow colours indicate is not clear.

Conflicting messages. Notice in Figure 3 that the 'Post and Send' button is currently enabled, even though the lights indicate that required information has not been entered. In the current implementation, the user is being simultaneously told that the form can and cannot be submitted. The labelling of this button itself is confusing enough: why 'post' *and* 'send'?

Labelling and placement of the lights. The lights are labelled 1 to 6, yet the tabs are not numerically labelled. This will require the user to determine the tab indicated by the number. Furthermore, the form is much larger than the image shown here and the lights are located a long way from the tabs they represent, thereby increasing the cognitive burden on the user.

You might like to start your own collection of misleading or confusing metaphors. But be careful to distinguish where the metaphor itself is the problem and where it is the implementation that causes difficulties. Perhaps you could discuss them with fellow students or colleagues, using FirstClass conferencing or at a tutorial.

4 | Interaction paradigms

4.1 | Review of the Set Book reading

STUDY NOTE

This section complements and extends Section 2.5 in the Set Book. If you have not already read Section 2.5 of the Set Book, then I suggest that you do so before reading any further.

Interaction paradigms represent different ways of thinking about an interaction. They therefore inform the second aspect of a conceptual model: how the product should behave. Instead of concentrating only on one user and her desktop personal computer, we can now envisage interactivity through a whole range of styles – for example, ubiquitous computing, tangible bits and attentive environments.

Review Question 10

Ubiquitous computing is sometimes regarded as synonymous with 'mobility'. Consider a mobile phone or personal digital assistant. In what ways does this device not conform to the idea of ubiquitous computing?

Not all the paradigms introduced here are widely available as yet. For example, ubiquitous computing and wearable computers are becoming more viable for the general public (see Box 2 for an example of wearable computing). On the other hand, tangible bits are not very common. To give you a better appreciation of what this interaction paradigm can offer, the next computer activity requires you to play two videos, each of which illustrates an application that has been built using the tangible bits paradigm. At the moment, tangible interfaces are mostly found in the research labs, but they are a good illustration of how different interaction could become in the near future.

ACTIVITY

Computer Activity 2: Tangible user interfaces

This activity will take approximately 45 minutes.

This activity gives you the opportunity to see some applications based on the tangible bits interaction paradigm.

Box 2: Wearable computing

The MIT/IDEO project is a joint effort between the Massachusetts Institute of Technology's Media Lab and IDEO Product Development. Using a scenario-driven process, the groups converged on two tales involving very different individuals: Kio and Guy. The scenarios explore the personal significance of wearable computing and try to understand how a single core technology could be utilized and interpreted in various ways.

The technologies that the scenarios describe are from the not too distant future. The intent of this project is to map, from a user perspective, where these technologies could go and to provide some guidance in their application.

Kio is a 19-year-old student at MIT; Guy is a 54-year-old Director of Oriental Antiquities with Sotheby's. They both have a set of wearables that allow them to interact with computer technology. This set comprises a ring, a wand, and a video interface (see photos below). Each has been designed to suit the wearer, i.e. Kio's set is bright and fashionable (indeed, she has ten different rings), while Guy's is more business-like.

Some images of wearable computing, from the MIT/IDEO website

The rings allow the wearer to control the interface, e.g. by increasing volume, altering the wearer's level of accessibility (i.e. when interruptions will be allowed). The pen can be used to write on any surface, including in mid-air, while the video interface allows images to be projected onto spectacles or the eye. All the functionality is driven from the base unit. Kio's is worn in a small rucksack around her waist, while Guy's is a slim pack that he wears on his belt. The base unit contains the central processor, memory, short/long range wireless communications, and a power unit to keep the system running.

Both individuals are very keen on their wearable sets. As Guy says: 'I don't even think about "wearing" my computer anymore, it's gotten to be as natural as wearing a watch (which, by the way, I no longer do). I imagine that the next step will be having my computer become a part of my body.'

ACTIVITY

Computer Activity 3: The design challenge of pervasive computing

This activity will take approximately one hour.

Read the paper 'The design challenge of pervasive computing' by John Thackara, which can be found on the course DVD. This paper sends a warning message about the situation we find ourselves in regarding technology. The author sketches a role for interaction design that would help avoid the kind of negative implications of life in a world with pervasive technology.

Outline this role.

COMMENT

You may find this a fairly pessimistic view of the world around us, but the main point is that interaction design can make the future better. Thackara points out that interaction design is about the 'why' as well as the 'how' of our daily interactions using computers. He claims that interaction design creates value in three ways: by designing new ways to connect with others; by allowing us richer and more varied forms of interaction, and by emphasising service and flow. He suggests that the last of these will change emphasis from us regarding ourselves as developers of products to becoming deliverers of service instead.

5 From conceptual models to physical design

5.1 Review of the Set Book reading

> **STUDY NOTE**
>
> This section complements and extends Section 2.6 in the Set Book. If you have not already read Section 2.6 of the Set Book, then I suggest that you do so before reading any further.

Section 2.6 describes briefly how a final product evolves through an iterative process involving the prototyping and evaluation of ideas and provisional designs. Each stage can be iterated many times until all the questions have been asked (and answered), all the assumptions have been identified, and so on. This topic will be covered in more practical depth in Unit 4 of this block.

Review Question 11

Section 2.6 suggests four possible initial passes through the iterative process of design, each in more depth. What are these four passes?

Review Question 12

Even though the focus of early iterations will be on identifying conceptual models, some issues concerned with physical design may arise. Name some of these issues, and explain why they might arise at this early stage.

ACTIVITY 5

Refer back to the Tokairo case study in Block 1, Unit 3. The description there doesn't specify the details of the iteration that they went through in designing the system. However, the participants talk about brainstorming, considering alternatives and using examples as inspiration. Throughout, the users and their needs guided deliberations.

How did the design at Tokairo emerge from this process? Is there a clear boundary between conceptual model development and physical design?

COMMENT

Many of the team's design decisions were driven by what they had learned about the user base, i.e. that they would be tired at the end of a shift, and wanting to get home. This meant that the interaction needed to be simple, flexible and familiar. These principles drove the choice of worksheet metaphor, i.e. that it would be like a lottery ticket, and the choice of interaction paradigm, i.e. one user with one computer. Having made these decisions, the idea was prototyped and screen shots captured. This prototype embodied the proposed conceptual model.

The process from conceptual model to physical design was not clearly defined, which is often the case in commercial projects. The prototype was used as a discussion tool, and then the details iteratively evolved. The principles identified early on were carried through both conceptual design and physical design.

References

Dorst, K. (2003) *Understanding Design*, BIS Publishers, Amsterdam.

Johnson, J. and Henderson, A. (2002) 'Conceptual models: begin by designing what to design', *Interactions*, Vol. 9, No. 1, January/February, pp. 25–32.

Marcus, A. (2000) 'User interface design for a vehicle navigation system', *Information Appliances and Beyond* (ed. Eric Bergman), Morgan Kaufman, pp. 205–255.

Unit learning outcomes

Having studied this unit, you should now be able to do the following:

LO1: Explain what is meant by the problem space for an intended product. This was discussed in Section 1 of this unit. If you are unsure about this, then look at pages 36 to 39 in the Set Book and have another go at Activity 1.

LO2: Define what a conceptual model is, and say what it is not. If you are unsure about what a conceptual model is and what it is not, then revisit Section 2.3 of this unit and have another look at Activities 2 and 3 and Computer Activity 1.

LO3: Provide and recognise examples of two different kinds of conceptual model: activity-based and object-based. If you are unsure about this, then re-read pages 41 to 53 in the Set Book, and associated activities. We will be returning to look in more detail at the idea of conceptual models in Unit 4.

LO4: Discuss the pros and cons of using interface metaphors as conceptual models. This was discussed on pages 55 to 60 of the Set Book. If you are unsure, then return to these pages and associated activities.

LO5: Describe different interaction paradigms and give examples of each. If you are still unsure of this, then re-read pages 60 to 64 of the Set Book and Section 4 of this unit. Computer Activity 2 shows you examples of a less common form of interaction paradigm, which will help you.

LO6: Outline the relationship between conceptual design and physical design. If you are unsure of this then take another look at Section 5 of this unit and pages 64 to 68 of the Set Book.

These contribute to the course learning outcomes as illustrated below.

Linking the unit learning outcomes to the course learning outcomes

Unit learning outcomes	Course learning outcomes
LO1, LO2	KU2: Define key terms used in interaction design
LO3, LO4, LO5, LO6	CS4: Produce a low-fidelity prototype for an interactive product based upon a simple list of interaction design principles
LO5, LO6	KS2: Communicate effectively to peers and specialists about requirements, design, and evaluation activities relating to interactive products.

Comments on review questions

REVIEW QUESTION 1 ....

If a designer begins by considering the physical aspects of an envisaged product, and maybe the technology to be used, then usability goals can easily be overlooked.

You may feel that the Tokairo case study in Block 1 is a counter-example to this position because they decided on the input and output devices early on. However, they did consider other possibilities and discuss user requirements, and their decision was based on experience and a good understanding of the intended users. In this case, then, the exploration of the problem space was very short.

REVIEW QUESTION 2 ....

The central activities are clarifying your usability and user experience goals, and explicating your assumptions.

REVIEW QUESTION 3 ....

The three sets of questions identified in Section 2.2 (page 38) are:

▶ Are there problems with an existing product? If so what are they? Why do you think there are problems?

▶ Why do you think your proposed ideas might be useful? How do you envision people integrating your proposed design with how they currently do things in their everyday or working lives?

▶ How will your proposed design support people in their activities? In what way does it address an identified problem or extend current ways of doing things? Will it really help?

REVIEW QUESTION 4 ....

The Set Book (page 36) suggests three approaches to exploring the problem space:

▶ Articulate the assumptions and claims about why developing such a product is a good idea.

▶ Conceptualise what you want to create and why, e.g. by considering different possible conceptual models.

▶ Think through how your product will support people in their everyday or working lives.

This last approach is addressed by the third set of questions identified in Section 2.2 of the Set Book.

REVIEW QUESTION 5 ....

The definition given is that a conceptual model is 'a description of the proposed system in terms of a set of integrated ideas and concepts about what it should do, behave and look like, that will be understandable by the users in the manner intended'. There are three main aspects which need describing: what the product should do, how it should behave and what it should look like.

REVIEW QUESTION 6 ....

The two main kinds of conceptual model are those based on activities and those based on objects.

REVIEW QUESTION 7 ....

Interface metaphors allow people to talk about what they are doing in terms they are familiar with, which gives them more confidence.

REVIEW QUESTION 8 ....

Designers sometimes take the metaphor too literally and try to design an interface that matches the characteristics of the metaphorical item. Instantiating the metaphor literally in an interface often leads to contradictions with the original item, and this can cause confusion rather than illumination.

Metaphors can be too constraining, both of the designer by not providing useful functionality, and of the user by blinding them to the existence of useful functionality.

Metaphors can lead to conflicts with design principles or to the literal translation of designs that were originally bad and have not been improved.

Finally, it is argued by some that use of metaphors limits the designer's imagination.

REVIEW QUESTION 9 ....

The interface metaphor potentially informs all three aspects of a conceptual model: what the product does, how it behaves, and what it looks like.

REVIEW QUESTION 10 ....

A mobile phone or PDA is a mobile device, yet ubiquitous computing is not simply about making devices portable. The intention with the ubiquitous paradigm is that technology be integrated into the environment. Mobile devices are (generally) not integrated into the environment but are carried around.

REVIEW QUESTION 11 ....

The first pass should involve thinking about the problem space and identifying some initial user requirements.

The second pass involves more extensive information gathering about user requirements.

A third pass should continue explicating user requirements and thinking through possible conceptual models.

A fourth pass might involve user-centred methods to flesh-out some of the possible models identified.

REVIEW QUESTION 12 ....

Many issues will need to be addressed at an early stage (although they can be changed later). These issues include: the way information is to be presented and interacted with at the interface; what combinations of media to use; the kind of feedback that will be provided, and so on. More are listed on page 65 of the Set Book.

These are addressed now in order to produce a concrete interactive prototype.

Unit 2: Choosing interaction devices

CONTENTS

Introduction to Unit 2

In Block 3 Unit 1 I explained the pivotal role of conceptual models in interaction design. In particular I emphasised the importance of creating the conceptual model before the physical design. In Chapter 2 of the Set Book it states that one of the issues that needs to be addressed when making the transition from conceptual model to physical design is:

> What combination of input and output devices to use (e.g. whether to use speech, keyboard plus mouse, handwriting recognition)

Source: Preece et al. (2002) p. 65

In this unit we will consider this particular issue in detail. The course team consider it to be of sufficient importance to include a dedicated unit because when you are trying to understand the problem space in order to identify your assumptions, it is easy to forget this issue, assuming your interactive product will inevitably use a keyboard and mouse.

To remind yourself about understanding the problem space see Block 3 Unit 1, Section 1.

In this unit I will encourage you to challenge this assumption, considering the particular requirements of your interactive product and how these can be best met by the various interaction devices (input and output devices) that are available.

The kind of interaction devices chosen can affect the user experience, and hence influence whether or not the user experience goals are met. We are not interested here in the internal workings of the devices, but consider them just from the point of view of how they affect interaction. We will discuss some of the interaction devices you have already met in Block 2 Unit 1. There the discussion focused on disability issues, while in this unit we are concerned with considering alternative interaction devices that may be appropriate for any user.

ACTIVITY 1

Figure 1 illustrates a personal digital assistant (PDA). This PDA has a calendar, memo pad, clock and various other standard functions.

The PDA has a small LCD screen, plus a stylus and a small number of buttons. The stylus is used for either writing on the screen or selecting options displayed on the screen. There is also a beeper that sounds when the pen is used to select an option on the screen.

Why do you think each of these interaction devices has been chosen? What alternatives to this design might have been possible?

Figure 1   A personal digital assistant (PDA)

COMMENT

I think the combination of stylus and screen has been chosen partly because they are similar to a pencil and writing pad – a familiar combination for most users. Also, because they take up less space than a keyboard and screen. (The problem with keyboards is that once they are reduced in size they become slower to use, because the keys are smaller and closer together.) However, this device might not be appropriate if the user suffers from poor motor control or is using the PDA in an unstable environment, as it requires the stylus to be positioned very precisely. In this case, a larger device, possibly with a full-size keyboard or speech input, might be better.

It would have been possible to produce the PDA without any physical buttons (apart from possibly the on/off switch), but the designers chose not to do this. This was probably because pressing physical buttons is usually quicker than tapping the screen with a stylus, so they identified a few frequently used functions (such as switching to the calendar option) and created some buttons for these. This made the PDA larger, but as with every aspect of design, there was a trade-off to be made; here it was speed of use versus size.

The PDA also has a beeper which sounds when the stylus touches the screen. This was probably included to improve the feedback – with physical buttons there is usually a click that accompanies the successful pressing of the button, but this does not happen when selecting a screen option with a stylus, so a beep fulfils the same function. Otherwise the user may be unsure whether or not the option has been successfully selected. However, the use of sound could be intrusive, for example if the PDA is used during a meeting. For this type of situation, the designers have made it possible to switch the beeper off.

Issues concerned with disabilities were discussed in Block 2 Unit 1.

To remind yourself of the feedback design principle, see Block 1 Unit 2, Section 2.

The discussion of interaction devices in this unit is organised according to the classification illustrated in Figure 2.

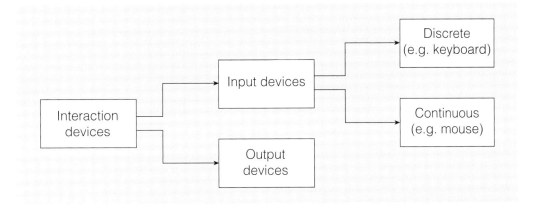

Figure 2   Classification of interaction devices

This discussion includes examples of interaction devices, consideration of issues around the choice of interaction devices, and lists of questions that need answering when you are choosing the most appropriate interaction devices for a particular context. It is not possible to consider every possible interaction device in this unit, as there are too many and more are being developed all the time. However, the purpose of this unit is to encourage you to approach the choice of devices in a reflective and analytical way, so not being comprehensive does not detract from this intent. In addition, interactive products such as MP3 players and mobile telephones are often fashion statements, so their appearance is as important to their users as their usability. In this unit we concentrate on the usability and functionality of products as enhanced by the choice of appropriate interaction devices, rather than on their appearance.

In addition, there are two substantial computer-based activities. The first asks you to explore the latest developments in interaction devices, looking at areas such as augmented reality, and the second asks you to explore the particular issues relating to users with special needs, building on the discussion both in this unit and in Block 2 Unit 1.

What you need to study this unit

You do not need the Set Book for this unit, but you will need the following course components:

▶ this book
▶ the course DVD.

You will need your computer and Internet connection for some of the activities.

How to study this unit

This unit involves studying the following teaching material, activities and review questions.

Choosing interaction devices

1.1 Interaction devices as tools

When you are hanging shelves on the wall in a house, you need to make a number of decisions about the tools to use. For example, you might choose the size of a screwdriver. This depends upon the size of screw you are using, which in turn depends upon the way in which you will use the shelf. If you are going to put a set of printed encyclopedias on the shelf, then those screws need to be stronger and more firmly fixed in the wall than if you intend to display some light ornaments. Thus the choice of tool depends upon the precise nature of the task being carried out.

What would happen if you have weak arms? Maybe you'd use an electric screwdriver, which would require less physical strength. What if you are working in a small bedroom and have a respiratory complaint, like asthma? You'd probably use a facemask to limit the dust inhaled. Thus the choice of tool also depends upon the characteristics of the user and the environment in which the user is working.

In a similar way, when we use an interactive product we want to achieve something. For example, we may want to make a phone call, enter text, draw a picture, access information or fly an aeroplane. Our choice of interaction devices is crucial to how well we can achieve these goals. Thus, writing a manual using a mouse is likely to be slow and frustrating, and drawing plans for an aircraft using a keyboard virtually impossible.

In order to choose between interaction devices, you need to ask the right questions. Some of these questions are driven by the constraints of the technology and others by the uses to which the technology will be put. In Sections 3 and 4 we will consider some of the key questions that you should ask when choosing input and output devices. These questions are only a subset of those that you will need to ask, as every situation depends upon the user's goals, the characteristics of the task, the types of user and the environment in which the devices are being used. These will have been uncovered during the requirements activity.

1.2 Why study interaction devices?

Think about the first computer you used. What was it like? Did you have a one-, two- or multiple-button mouse? What about a scrolling wheel? If you're older, you may even recall the days before the mouse became ubiquitous, perhaps even the use of paper tape for input and a slow, poor-quality, dot-matrix printer for output. Interactive products and interaction devices are more sophisticated nowadays, and it is possible to tailor the interaction experience far more closely to the task at hand, and the users involved.

The QWERTY keyboard, screen and mouse are the standard set of interaction devices available for desktop PCs. If the PC is to be used for playing games, then a steering wheel or joystick might be added to the configuration. But consider other interactive products: an ATM (cash machine) might use a touch-screen and/or a limited keypad control input and output; for mobile phones a different kind of screen and a different keypad, are used; and for a video cassette recorder a remote control box is now common, again with a specialised keypad.

'Darn these hooves! I hit the wrong switch again!
Who designs these instrument panels, racoons?'

Different tasks, users and environments require different interaction devices. Choosing inappropriate devices can lead to user frustration, inefficiency, and all the things that interaction design is intended to avoid. Choosing appropriate devices can make all the difference. Box 1 gives two examples where using the right technology was particularly important.

For more information, see Partridge (1999).

Box 1: Why choosing interaction devices matters

There are circumstances in which choosing the correct device is essential.

Users may have particular requirements, so it is important to understand the users of the system, and the way in which they use the technology. For example, the messaging company Pitney Bowes carried out a survey of office workers in North America, Britain and Germany. One of the findings was that Europeans use communications technology very differently to North Americans. In particular, Europeans prefer direct contact using a mobile telephone rather than leaving voicemail messages. The opposite is true for North Americans.

The same difference is reinforced by the use of pagers: 20% of North Americans use pagers compared with about 5% of Europeans. The implications of these cultural differences are that the technology purchased by a company needs to take into account the way in which the employees will use it. Thus a European company may prefer to employ a secretary, so that their clients can speak directly to a person; but for North Americans, a voicemail system might suffice.

Or the task may have particular requirements. For example, in a large warehouse, if the boxes were not bar-coded, then the employees would need to type in all the details every time a box arrived or was dispatched. With a large warehouse having thousands of these transactions every day, doing this would be very time consuming and prone to error.

2 Input devices

The distinction between input and output devices is not as clear-cut as I have suggested. It is unusual to encounter a device that is purely one or the other. The keyboard is a good example of this: when you press a key, you receive tactile and audio feedback when the key clicks. Thus the keyboard is acting as both an input and output device. Keyboards are predominantly input devices, but this confirmatory feedback is a feature of good design as it confirms that the user has done what she intended.

In this section we look at two categories of input device.

1 *Keyboards, keypads and buttons*. There is a variety of types of keyboard and keypad. Individual buttons are also used extensively, particularly in embedded computer systems.

2 *Pointing devices*. This category is divided into indirect pointing devices, such as the mouse and joystick, and direct pointing devices, such as touch-screen and stylus-based systems.

For both categories we will consider what the particular devices can best be used for and how to choose between them. We finish by considering some of the more advanced input devices.

2.1 Keyboards, keypads and buttons

Keyboards, keypads and buttons are all **discrete input devices**. Discrete input devices can be used to enter discrete pieces of information, such as letters and numbers or commands. Thus a keyboard is good for typing documents and the 'on' key on your mobile telephone is good for executing the 'switch on telephone' command. None of these devices is ideally suited to continuous tasks such as dragging icons across the screen.

The most sophisticated form of discrete input device is the keyboard. The vast majority of keyboards for use in English-speaking countries have the QWERTY layout, the name being taken from the six keys in the top row of letters, starting from the left-hand side. The keyboard on your computer will almost certainly have this kind of layout. The QWERTY keyboard became an international standard in 1967. It has an interesting past, as Box 2 describes.

Box 2: An early keyboard

The keyboard is based upon the typewriter, which was first envisaged in 1711 by James Ranson who proposed a design for a machine with keys, rather like those on a harpsichord. Thus, using a typewriter was initially likened to playing a twin-keyboard harpsichord. One of the first actual keyboards was built in 1868 by Scholes, Gidden and Soulé to help overcome the forgery of handwritten railway tickets.

Rumour has it that the layout of the QWERTY keyboard was designed in order to prevent the mechanical keys of the typewriter from jamming. Commonly-paired letters are spaced far apart on the keyboard, which had the effect of slowing down the typists and hence averting the jam. Another tongue-in-cheek observation is that the letters to make up the word 'typewriter' are all in the top line.

For more information, see Baber (1997) and Tepper (1993).

Keyboards for other languages have different layouts, sometimes simply to add in characters with accents (e.g. é in French, Þ in Icelandic) or more extensive changes to allow easier entry of other scripts, as in the Russian keyboard shown in Figure 3.

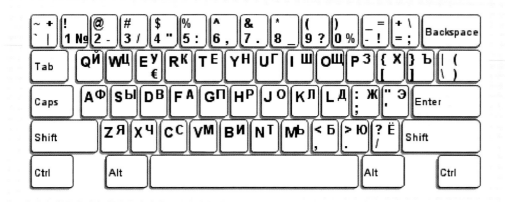

Figure 3   The Russian keyboard layout makes it easier to enter Cyrillic script

One of the disadvantages of QWERTY keyboards is that they can be over-elaborate, containing a range of keys that are rarely, if ever, used. If this is the case, it might be possible to develop a variation of the standard arrangement. For example, BigKeys make a range of keyboards with large keys. They find the extra room to enlarge the keys by removing keys that are unnecessary for the applications the keyboard is intended for. For example, Figures 4 and 5 show a BigKeys keyboard aimed at young children. In order to make this attractive for children, in addition to having large keys with letters on, the letter keys also display simple illustrations. Other keyboards in the BigKeys range are popular with people with special needs such as vision problems or hand tremor who find large keys useful.

We also discussed BigKeys in Block 2 Unit 1.

Figure 4   The 'early learning' version of the BigKeys keyboard

Figure 5   Children using the 'early learning' version of the BigKeys keyboard

It is possible to move away from the QWERTY keyboard completely. Box 3 describes a different type of keyboard that you may come across.

Box 3: The chord keyboard

An alternative to the QWERTY keyboard is the chord keyboard, on which several keys are pressed at the same time in order to enter a single character. This is similar to playing a flute, where several keys must be pressed to produce a single note. Since many combinations can be produced with a small number of keys, few keys are required; so chord keyboards can be very small. Many chord keyboards can be operated with just one hand. Training is required to learn the finger combinations needed to use a chord keyboard. They can be very useful where space is limited, or where one hand is involved in some other task. Chord keyboards are also used for mail sorting and for recording transcripts of proceedings in law courts.

A chord keyboard is shown in Figure 6. Note that this is a left-handed keyboard layout (the thumb goes on one of the three coloured buttons while the palm of the hand rests on the pad on the right), and would be unsuitable for right-handed users.

Box 7.1 in the Set Book (page 208) describes a chord keyboard that was designed for use by underwater divers.

Figure 6   A chord keyboard

If you do not need the full range of alphanumeric keys, a keypad may be more appropriate. Many everyday devices, such as calculators and telephones, use keypads very successfully. An even simpler approach is to use individual buttons, as on burglar alarms and central heating controllers.

2.1.1   Choosing the correct keyboard, keypad and buttons

When you are choosing the most appropriate keyboard, consider the following questions.

▶ *What shape should the keyboard be?* If you decide to use a QWERTY keyboard, then there are some alternatives to consider. For example, Figure 7 illustrates a split keyboard designed to combat repetitive strain injury (RSI). It does this by allowing the hands to rest in a more natural position than a traditional keyboard allows.

▶ *What size do the keys need to be?* Keyboards are available with every size of key from the huge keys of the BigKeys keyboard series (Figure 4) down to the tiny keys used to achieve functionality with maximum portability on mobile devices (Figure 8).

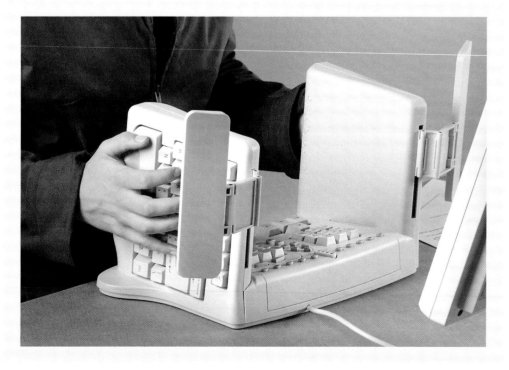

Figure 7   An alternative shape of keyboard

Figure 8   Keyboards for mobile or portable devices can be tiny

▶ *How robust does the keyboard need to be?* In difficult environments, such as
factories, ordinary keyboards can clog up with dirt and liquids. Membrane keyboards
solve this problem as they are sealed. Unfortunately they are flat, so they do not
provide the same tactile and audio feedback. Software needs to compensate for this.
Often such keyboards have software that detects if a key has accidentally been
pressed more than once under unlikely circumstances, and discards the repetitions.

The size and robustness of the keys (or buttons) also need to be considered if you decide
to use a keypad or individual buttons. In addition, you need to decide upon which keys
(or buttons) are required and how these should be labelled. If you own a scientific
calculator or a graphics calculator, you will appreciate that these can be complex tasks.

ACTIVITY 2

Suppose that a keyboard or keypad is to be used for a road survey, to assist in the task of
recording the number and types of vehicle that pass a particular roundabout. What type
of keyboard or keypad would you choose for this situation? Describe your choice in terms
of the following considerations:

▶   key size

▶   robustness

▶   the keys that are needed.

Assume that cost is not a consideration

COMMENT

In this discussion we assume that the keyboard or keypad is integrated into an interactive product with one or more complementary output devices.

▶ *Key size.* The keyboard or keypad would need to be easy to handle as there are unlikely to be any flat surfaces and the surveyors may be standing. Thus, it will need to be held in one hand, whilst the other hand does the typing. As a consequence, the keys will need to be reasonably large and the keyboard light to carry. However, because the product is a hand-held device it also needs to be small, and so the keys cannot be too large. This leads to a conflict which requires a carefully-designed compromise.

▶ *Robustness.* It will need to be robust as the work takes place out of doors with the possibility of rain or snow. It may also be dropped.

▶ *Keys that are needed.* As there is a relatively small number of different tasks, it might be worth restricting the number of keys and designing a special keypad. This would enable surveyors to enter data more quickly and accurately. Once they became proficient, it might be possible for the surveyor to keep their eyes on the road and not look repeatedly at the input device.

The simplest solution would be to have a keypad with a separate key for each type of vehicle being counted. This would mean that recording each vehicle would require a single key press.

2.2 | Pointing devices

A flick through any online or offline catalogue will show you a range of pointing devices. The ordinary computer mouse (now available in many styles to suit all tastes as shown in Figure 9) is the most common, and you are probably familiar with this device. You may also be familiar with some of the other devices available, e.g. joystick and touch-screen.

Pointing devices are **continuous input devices**. This means they are particularly good at tasks that cannot be split easily into a number of discrete steps, such as dragging icons across the screen or drawing informal sketches. The standard configuration of input devices for many computer systems is the keyboard and mouse. This works well, as the keyboard is a discrete input device and the mouse is a continuous input device.

There are two types of pointing device: indirect and direct. **Indirect pointing devices** require the user to move a screen cursor using a secondary device; **direct pointing devices** allow the user to point directly at the relevant position on the screen.

2.2.1   Types of indirect pointing devices

Some indirect pointing devices that are often seen are described here.

Mouse

A **mouse** is an input device that allows an individual to control a cursor or other pointer on the screen, see Figure 9. The mouse has one or more buttons on its surface which allow the user to select the item at the current cursor position. Underneath the mouse is a ball which translates movement of the mouse into movement of the cursor on the screen.

Figure 9   Computer mice available in custom shapes as promotional items

Joystick

A **joystick** is a lever mounted in a fixed base, see Figure 10. There are various types of joystick, including displacement and isometric joysticks. In **displacement joysticks**, the lever can be moved in two dimensions. Moving the lever in a particular direction causes the cursor to move and to continue moving in that direction. **Isometric joysticks** work in a similar way, but the lever is rigid and the pressure on the lever is translated into the necessary movement. Interaction designers often incorporate joysticks into game consoles, where they are used to control moving objects such as racing cars. Small joysticks are sometimes built into the keyboards of notebook computers (sometimes called 'nipple' or 'eraser head' joysticks due to their small size and shape).

Figure 10   This especially tough joystick is helpful for people with disabilities. If gripping the joystick is awkward, the user can choose instead to screw the yellow sponge-ball or the T-Bar onto the joystick spindle.

Trackball

A **trackball** is an inverted mouse: the user rotates the ball and the case is fixed. These are often incorporated into game consoles. Some people with limited finger movement find it easier to move a trackball than a mouse. Like mice, trackballs are available in different sizes and shapes to suit varying user needs. One example is shown in Figure 11.

Figure 11   This extra-large trackball was originally designed for children, but is also popular with people who have disabilities that affect their fingers.

Graphics tablet (or tablet)

A **graphics tablet** is a flat panel, see Figure 12. The cursor moves as the user moves a stylus or finger across the tablet. Graphics tablets are often used for creating drawings, as using them feels similar to creating a conventional drawing using a pencil and paper. Some portable computers have a small graphics tablet called a touch tablet (or touch pad). You roll your finger on this to move the cursor; to select an object you tap on the tablet, or press a button. Learning to use these devices requires more practice than does a conventional mouse, and users with limited dexterity often find them difficult to operate compared to using a mouse.

There is a great deal of variety in each of these devices. Almost every month a new variation comes out, so you might like to look in some of the recent computer magazines in order to find out what is happening now.

Figure 12   A graphics tablet with stylus

2.2.2   Types of direct pointing device

Some common direct pointing devices are described here.

Touch-screen

A **touch-screen** allows the user to input information and commands into an interactive product by touching buttons on the screen. For example, a system giving directions to visitors at a large exhibition may first present an overview of the exhibition layout in the form of a general map. Users touch the hall they wish to visit and the system presents a more detailed map of the chosen hall. Touch-screens on kiosks (as in Figure 13) are set up with big targets and are used by pointing with your finger.

Figure 13   A touch-screen used on a kiosk in the Tokairo case study

Pen system

A **pen system** uses a touch-screen but is set up for using a stylus (a pen) rather than a finger. Because the stylus is much smaller, pen systems can have much smaller targets and they are therefore seen frequently on PDAs (**Personal Digital Assistants**). Pen systems are also seen at check-outs in some stores, where the customer can 'sign' on the screen using a stylus rather than using pen on paper (Figure 14). Delivery companies sometimes ask for a signature that is written with a stylus on a touch-screen.

Figure 14   A touch-screen set up for signing at a check-out

Light pen

A **light pen** is a stylus that contains a photo receptor, see Figure 15. It works out where on a cathode ray tube (CRT) screen it is being pointed (see Section 3.1). It does this by detecting the tiny variations in intensity of the light emitted by the screen as the electron beam tracks horizontally and vertically across it. Light pens used to be quite common but have been overtaken by touch-screens and pen systems.

Figure 15   A light pen

2.2.3   Choosing the right pointing device

When you are choosing a pointing device (indeed any input device), you need to ensure you understand the context of use fully, as the following example illustrates.

> ... in a hospital, the image from an ultrasound-scanner was being manipulated using cross-hairs and cursor which were used to select part of the scan for enlargement. The cursor was controlled by a joystick, much to the frustration of the midwife, who kept overshooting the point of interest. Eventually, the joystick was replaced by a trackball. The overshoot persisted.
>
> This example, in which one interaction device was replaced by another, illustrates one response to these problems: to identify a specific symptom and to attempt to treat that. One might ask why a trackball was chosen. The principal reason is space. The interaction device is used on a piece of equipment mounted on a trolley, and there is a limited amount of space for the device to be positioned. However, the interaction device (whether joystick or trackball) is positioned behind the screen, to the left of the trolley. Given a right-handed midwife, operating the interaction device implies a reach across the screen, thus blocking the image, or an operation from behind the screen. In either case, there is a chance of overshooting the object of interest.
>
> Source: Baber (1997, pp. 3–4)

In this example the development team thought the joystick itself was the cause of the overshoot, whereas the actual problem was that the midwife obstructed the screen when reaching across to operate the joystick. In this situation, a pen system might have been better than a trackball, as it would have allowed the midwife to touch the point of interest on the screen with great accuracy, without obscuring the image or moving awkwardly.

When you are choosing the most appropriate pointing device, consider the following questions.

▶ *How easy to learn does the device need to be?* Direct pointing devices, such as a stylus, tend to be straightforward to use, as touching and pointing come naturally in a way that using an indirect pointing device, like a mouse, does not. Therefore, they are ideal in situations where a particular user may only operate the system once or twice, and cannot be expected to spend time learning to use it. This ease of use may be undermined if the software requires unnatural actions such as double-tapping.

▶ *How accurate does the device need to be?* The pointing device should reflect the degree of accuracy needed to carry out the task. Touch-screens are generally inaccurate; this is made worse if there is a build-up of dirt on the surface. Joysticks are also fairly inaccurate. When a device is inherently inaccurate, it is necessary to increase the size of the screen elements with which the user interacts. For example, buttons need to be larger. This can result in less room for text and graphics.

▶ *How much time will the user spend on the system?* Using a touch-screen for long periods can be tiring, as it requires the user to repeatedly lift an arm. This can be alleviated if the screen is horizontal or angled. Graphics tablets can be less tiring, as it is not necessary to keep lifting the hand. Also, the hand does not obscure the display. Joysticks require a wrist rest if they are used for lengthy periods. In contrast, the trackball is relatively comfortable to use, as the forearm can be rested on the table and the ball spun with the fingers.

▶ *How much space is there?* The trackball, joystick and touch tablet require very little room. At one time, some notebook computers came with miniature trackballs but these have now been largely abandoned in favour of 'nipple style' miniature joysticks and touch tables. Despite their small size, or possibly because of it, many users dislike them and carry a separate mouse.

▶ *How robust does the device need to be?* Touch-screens are often used for public-access systems, as they are easy to use and can be robust if sufficiently well built. Pen systems are not as good in these situations, as the stylus could be broken or stolen.

▶ *How manually dextrous is the user?* Some users, such as children and people with disabilities such as hand tremor, may find it difficult to use devices that require a high degree of accuracy. Therefore, such users may find a touch-screen easier to use than a mouse.

As you can see from this discussion, choosing pointing devices is not an exact science, as the appropriateness of a device is entirely dependent upon the circumstances in which it will be used. There is also a lot of disagreement in the research literature. This makes drawing any general conclusions about these devices extremely difficult.

I have included Figure 16 as a summary of some of the research findings on accuracy, speed and user preference. I have already considered accuracy; speed refers to cursor movement and data entry; user preference is self-explanatory. Unfortunately, the original experiments did not control all the relevant variables, such as the type of task being completed or the experience of the users. Consequently, you should only treat this chart as an indicator. The vertical axis reflects the ranking of the device, with 1 being the best and 7 the worst. Pen systems are omitted, but it seems likely that pen systems and light pens have similar characteristics.

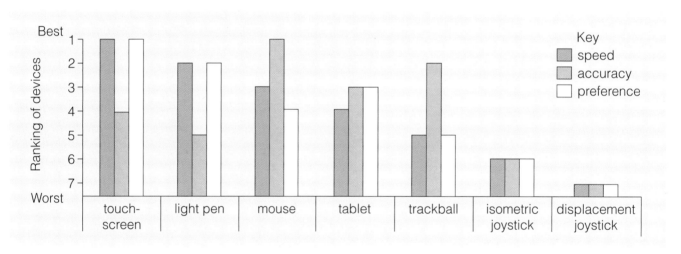

Figure 16   Comparison of pointing devices

ACTIVITY 3

A tourist information centre wants to design a system to provide information about accommodation and events in the town, that will be used by visitors of all ages. It will be located in the wall outside the tourist information centre, so that it can be accessed from the pavement when the centre is shut.

Consider the merits of each of the following pointing devices as a means of interacting with this system:

▶ touch-screen

▶ trackball

▶ mouse.

Refer to the users, the tasks they will be carrying out, and the environment in which they will be using the system. In particular, consider the following points.

Users
- ▶ user attitude to the device (preference)
- ▶ how easy the device is to learn to use

Task
- ▶ the accuracy needed
- ▶ the speed needed
- ▶ the total amount of time spent using the system to accomplish this task

Environment
- ▶ the robustness of the device
- ▶ the amount of space available.

COMMENT

Touch-screen. It is easy to learn to use touch-screens, and the user attitude to them is good: these are both advantages for use in a public-access system. However, they are not very accurate, so the screen buttons will need to be large. This will restrict the amount of information that can be displayed at one time and could result in having a large number of screens; for example, one for each hotel or guest house. This should be acceptable, so long as there are not too many or there is a good search facility. Speed is important because the user may well be in a hurry, particularly if the system is not under cover and it is raining. The total time spent using the system will be quite short, so arm ache should not be a problem for most users; however, it could cause difficulties for those with muscular problems. Touch-screens are robust, which is necessary for a damp and dirty environment. Space is probably not an issue, but touch-screens are very compact.

Trackball. Trackballs are robust and take up very little space. Young people are familiar with trackballs on games machines, so they may find these more intuitive than non-games players. Other users tend to have a less positive attitude to trackballs. They are slower to use – moving to the precise position on the screen can be laborious – but they are more accurate than touch-screens. Thus, there is a trade-off between large screen buttons increasing the speed of use and smaller screen buttons increasing the amount of information that can be represented on the screen.

Mouse. Many users will be familiar with the mouse as it is so widely used. It is more accurate than both the touch-screen and the trackball. This means that more information could be represented on the screen. However, the mouse would not be suitable for outdoor use because it is not robust and could be stolen.

Review Question 1

This section has introduced two different kinds of input devices: keyboards or keypads, and pointing devices. Briefly describe one example of each, and suggest an example application for which it would be appropriate.

2.3 Alternative approaches to input

There is a lot of exciting research work in the area of input devices. As an example of this, Box 4 describes an eye-tracking system. A few of the other important areas are described on the followng pages.

For more information, see the websites of SensoMotoric Instruments http://www.smi.de/ and Tobii Technology http://www.tobii.se/ .

Box 4: Eye tracking

How could you operate a computer by moving your eyes? The answer is to use eye-tracking technology.

Figure 17(a) illustrates one possible configuration for this technology. This shows a traditional head-mounted eye-tracking device from SensoMotoric Instruments which records eye movements based on the reflections of the pupil and the cornea. The eye tracker uses two small cameras (the eye camera and the scene camera) mounted on a bicycle helmet. No physical contact is made with the participant's eye. An infrared light shines into the participant's eye so that the front surface of the eyeball is illuminated. This produces two effects: a bright pupil and corneal reflection.

Figure 17(b) shows a Tobii Technology 1750 non-intrusive eye-tracking device with a small video camera positioned at the bottom of the monitor. The user is not required to wear headgear of any kind, and there are no other hardware components to cause distraction.

The user moves a cursor by simply looking at the place that is of interest. If it is a button, then either blinking or looking at the button for a prolonged period can 'press' it.

This technology has to overcome several problems, including the following:

▶ infrared light from other sources, such as the sun, shining into the eye

▶ the user wearing glasses or contact lenses

▶ the image being blocked if the user moves a hand between the camera and the eye

▶ the calibration of these systems is often difficult

▶ considerable user concentration is required to use the system effectively.

This technology is also used to analyse where on a screen users are focusing their attention during evaluation sessions.

Evaluation is discussed in Block 4.

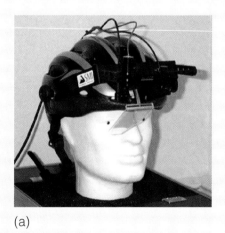 

(a)   (b)

Figure 17   Two examples of eye-tracking technology: (a) SensoMotoric Instruments, (b) Tobii Technology

2.3.1 Gesture

Gesture is widely used in communication between people. We gesticulate, shake hands and move objects around. Gestural interfaces moved from the laboratory into the home with the launch of the Sony PlayStation Eye Toy in the summer of 2003. The Eye Toy is a small camera that sits above or below the player's television, and then allows them to be 'part of' the game and use gestures to control it. Figure 18 shows the camera and an image from the game.

(a)   (b)

Figure 18   (a) The Sony PlayStation Eye Toy camera, (b) the player in the middle of the screen uses gestures to control the game

2.3.2 Iris and fingerprint recognition

Security is an important issue when carrying out activities such as withdrawing cash from an ATM or entering a building containing military secrets. Maintaining security requires some kind of password or recognition system to be in place. One approach to this is to have a system that can recognise people based upon their fingerprints or their irises (the coloured part of the eye). An example is shown in Figure 19.

Figure 19   Iris recognition equipment in use at Amsterdam Schiphol International Airport. The system compares a person's iris template with their pre-registered version to verify identity.

2.3.3 Handwriting recognition

The popularity of hand-held computers based around pen systems has meant that handwriting recognition has become an important approach to entering data. As each person has different handwriting, the system must be trained to recognise each user's handwriting, so this approach is most appropriate for single-user systems. In addition, when we join letters together, we shape the letters differently according to the letters that come before and after. For this reason, the majority of recognition systems insist that the user form each letter individually or use a specific alphabet such as that used by the Graffiti® system illustrated in Figure 20. This can make writing rather slow.

Letter	Stroke	Letter	Stroke	Letter	Stroke	Letter	Stroke
A	Λ	B	ß	C	C	D	D
E	Ɛ	F	Γ	G	G	H	h
I	i	J	J	K	K	L	L
M	⋔	N	N	O	O	P	p
Q	q	R	R	S	S	T	✝
U	U	V	V	W	W	X	X
Y	ɏ	Z	Z				

Figure 20   The letter forms for Graffiti 2, used by palmOne hand-held devices

2.3.4   Speech recognition

Speech recognition packages have been developing rapidly over the past decade. It is now common to have telephone answering systems that respond to voice input. As with handwriting recognition, there are a number of problems that need to be overcome. These include different regional accents, pauses and meaningless utterances such as 'err' and 'umm', the vast range of possible words and our tendency to use words incorrectly. For these reasons, the error rate for such systems is quite high. However, they do have their benefits, particularly for constrained situations where only a limited selection of words is required, such as some telephone voice response systems or as dictation systems for people who find it difficult or painful to use a keyboard.

For users who produce large quantities of written material, it may be worth the investment of time to train the system to be able to recognise their speech. However, do not confuse voice recognition and speech recognition systems. The former can identify an individual from their voice (and may be used for password or security applications), while the latter are able to translate the spoken word into the written form.

Review Question 2

This section has introduced four alternative forms of input: gesture, iris and fingerprint recognition, handwriting recognition and speech recognition. Which of these is discrete and which is continuous?

3 Output devices

In this section we will look at four categories of output device.

▶ *Screens.* Screens are the most common category of output device. They are very versatile and are excellent for displaying complex visual data.

▶ *Loudspeakers.* These are needed for the inclusion of sound, such as music or speech.

▶ *Simple output devices.* Many systems have a selection of lights, dials and buzzers, often indicating the status of the system.

▶ *Printers.* Many applications that run on interactive devices require some form of paper-based output to be generated, i.e. printed out.

We finish by looking briefly at more advanced technologies, such as head-up displays, head-mounted displays and stereoscopic displays.

Output devices designed specifically for accessibility were discussed in Block 2. Here the focus is on more general output devices.

Other accessible technologies were discussed in Block 2 Unit 1.

3.1 Screens

Screens can represent a wide variety of visual elements. Even people with visual impairments generally like to read from a screen if they can, frequently using magnifying devices or magnifying software such as ZoomText™ to help them do so.

There are two main types of screen technology commonly available: the **cathode ray tube** and the **liquid crystal display**.

▶ *The raster-scan cathode ray tube (CRT).* This technology is similar to that of the television and is traditionally used for desktop computers. At one time, CRTs were prone to flickering, but advances in technology mean that they are now the device of choice for a cheap-and-cheerful computer system, and for applications where very large screens with accurate colour rendition are essential (such as high-end graphics workstations).

▶ *The liquid crystal display (LCD).* LCDs are much smaller, thinner and lighter than CRTs with the same visible area. They also consume less power. At first, they were mostly used in portable devices, but advances in technology have made them affordable for ordinary desk-top use.

3.1.1 Choosing the right screen

As with much technology in the area, the quality of screens is constantly improving. However, several issues must be taken into account, including the following.

▶ *How detailed does the image need to be?* The **resolution** indicates the amount of detail that can be represented on the screen. Resolution is defined in terms of the number of pixels (picture elements) per unit area. Thus, a screen may have 600 dpi (dots per inch). The higher this figure, the higher the resolution – and the smaller the pixels on the screen. In some cases high resolution is essential, for example if you manipulate photographs. In other cases it is less important, for example if you work mainly with text. Screen resolution is sometimes lower than the resolution of paper (depending upon your printer), so if the screen resolution is too low you may find users print out the screen content.

▶ *How many colours are needed?* The number of colours available can vary from two (black and white) to millions. Although black and white can be very successful, for example earlier versions of the Palm Pilot or mobile phones, the trend is generally to move to colour as soon as it is affordable.

▶ *How large does the screen need to be?* By convention, screens have been measured across the diagonal, with common sizes for desktop monitors being 17, 19 and 21 inches. As the price of screens is falling, users are tending to opt for larger displays. Larger displays have many advantages, as more visual information can be displayed. Larger text can also be displayed, which is an advantage for the visually impaired. Such equipment has been standard for many years for graphic designers. There is also a large market for much smaller screens. In particular, these are used for small portable devices, such as hand-held computers and mobile phones. These always use LCDs, as it is difficult to make small portable CRTs.

▶ *Does the screen need to be portable?* CRTs need an electrical supply and are very heavy. Thus CRTs cannot be used for portable devices. LCDs are battery operated and lightweight. Also the batteries last a reasonable length of time. Thus they are suitable for portable devices.

▶ *How much space is there?* Increasingly LCDs are used instead of CRTs for desktop PCs as they take up less space. This can be important in a crowded office environment.

There are other variables to take into account, but those discussed above are the main ones.

ACTIVITY 4

Specify a screen type for the following interactive products. Describe your choice in terms of technology (LCD or CRT), resolution, screen size, portability and available space.

▶ *A mobile telephone.* The screen will indicate when the telephone is connected to the network, the number being dialled, and so on. It is likely to be used in all types of situation, including at night and in the rain.

▶ *A meeting room display screen.* The screen will be used to display complex three-dimensional graphics in a design studio. It is likely that several people will want to look at the design at any one moment.

COMMENT

▶ *A mobile telephone.* The most appropriate type of screen is the LCD. Such screens are physically light and they consume batteries increasingly slowly, as battery technology develops. Resolution can be quite low if the screen is only used to display text and numbers, but needs to be higher if photographs and icons are to be displayed. The screen size will need to be quite small as the device is portable, but increasingly phone manufacturers are experimenting with screens of different sizes for different uses.

▶ *A meeting room display screen.* Traditionally, large CRTs with a high resolution and millions of colours have been used for this type of context. This is because the screen does not need to be portable, and it is sometimes necessary to look at very complex and colourful images. These CRTs take up a lot of room. If space is a problem, it might be worth investigating a large LCD display.

3.2 Printers

As with screens, there are many different varieties of printer available. Some of them stand alone, and some may be integrated into the interactive device. For example, the printer that produces the receipt slip from an ATM (cash machine) is very different from the plotter used in graphics studios to produce high-quality presentation drawings.

There are two different types of printer most commonly associated with interactive devices: inkjet printers and laser printers.

▶ **Inkjet printers** put an image on paper using tiny jets of ink.

▶ **Laser printers** put an image on the paper using static electricity.

From a user's point of view the main difference between the two kinds is based on quality, although this is becoming less true as technology improves. The laser printer produces better quality print than the ink jet, but the ink can take longer to dry than on a laser-printed document. For most applications the inkjet is usually good enough and is noticeably cheaper.

The questions to consider when choosing a printer are very similar to those for a screen:

▶ *What resolution of image is required?* This is usually measured in dots per inch (referred to as dpi). The higher the dpi the better quality is the printed document.

▶ *Is colour needed?* Or will black and white output be sufficient?

▶ *What size of paper is needed?* For example, an architects' office needs to print out plans up to size A1 or A0 in some cases, while an A4 printer is usually sufficient for a standard office application. Printers attached to cash desks in a shop or portable printers need to be much smaller.

▶ *Does the printer need to be portable?* Laser printers tend to be much heavier than inkjet printers.

▶ *How much space is there?* Laser printers also tend to be larger than inkjet printers.

3.3 Loudspeakers

The use of sound is becoming increasingly sophisticated as technology improves. In the 1980s many computers were able to beep, but that was all. Now most interactive products have sound output, and good-quality speakers are available. These can be used to reproduce speech, music and sound effects. Many products also have microphones (the 'matching' input device) that allow sound to be entered into the system, for example recording your own ring tone for your mobile phone.

When you are choosing loudspeakers, you should consider how the user is going to use them. For example, if you are designing a product for a composer who wants to create an intricate piece of music, then the quality of the loudspeakers needs to be high. In contrast, if the user is only using them for the sound effects generated on his PC by Windows, then the speakers can be of a lower quality. Surprisingly, the quality of speakers is often unrelated to their price, especially at smaller sizes. If you can, arrange to try them in the environment in which they will be used.

3.4 Simple output devices

There is a variety of simple output devices that can be used in addition to (or instead of) a screen and loudspeakers. The most common of these are lights, dials and buzzers. These devices are cheap and extremely useful.

Lights often indicate whether a product is on or off. For example, your computer probably has a light that indicates when the power is on. Lights can also be used in a more sophisticated manner. For example, some mobile telephones have a light emitting diode (LED) that is red when the telephone is charging and green when charging is complete. (This can be a problem for those users who are colour blind.) It is also quite common for mobile telephones to have a flashing LED indicating when network reception is strong.

Issues with colour-blind users were discussed in Block 2 Unit 1.

Some products use displays where each character is made up of seven LEDs, such as the digits in the answer phone display illustrated in Figure 21. Different combinations of the LEDs are used to display different numbers and letters. These are called seven-segment displays.

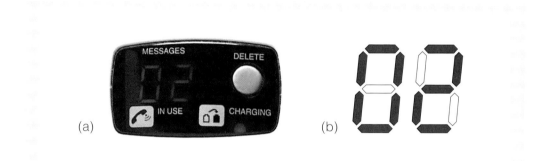

(a)   (b)

Figure 21   Display panel of an answer phone device. (a) The display uses two seven-segment displays to show the number of messages received. (b) Each digit of the display is made up of seven LEDS.

Dials and gauges are widely used to indicate levels. Examples include the speedometer dial in a car or the battery-level gauge on a hand-held computer.

Simple sound output, such as a buzzer, is often used to attract the attention of the user. For example, some bread-makers indicate the next stage in a cycle with a beep, so the cook does not need to keep checking for the right time to add the next lot of ingredients.

A common approach to output is to combine a number of simple output devices to communicate more sophisticated output. For example, some products combine gauges, lights and sound. Many microwave ovens indicate that they have completed an operation by using a buzzer, switching off the internal light and displaying a digital clock. Users are thus given multiple outputs to tell them that the process is finished. Figure 22 shows a more complex and ambitious use of lights, dials, gauges and buzzers.

Figure 22   An aircraft cockpit

One issue that you need to consider when choosing between lights, dials and gauges is whether the data can be represented more effectively in analogue or digital form. A single light is effective for representing **discrete data**. Thus a single light can be used to indicate if a product is on or off. In contrast, a dial or gauge is better for representing data that can have a large number of different states.

The issue of information display is revisited in Block 3 Unit 4, Section 3.4.

In addition, lights have a number of characteristics.

► *Colour.* You may need a light that is a particular colour or is able to change colours.

► *Frequency of flashing.* Flashing lights can be useful for attracting the attention of the user. A light that can flash at different frequencies may be useful. However, flashing lights can be irritating.

► *Brightness.* It may be necessary to alter the brightness of the light. For example, a dashboard light needs to be adjusted as night falls.

Buzzers can be particularly effective if users are looking away from the product. For example, the choice of a buzzer that sounds when a driver opens a car door with the headlights left switched on is a good one, because the user will not be looking at the dashboard. Buzzers are also used as an additional form of feedback. For example, selecting a button on a touch-screen gives no tactile feedback, so the device often beeps instead.

ACTIVITY 5

Suggest how two lights and a gauge might be used as feedback on a digital camera. Specify the lights in terms of colour, brightness and frequency of flashing. Suggest how the gauge might be displayed.

COMMENT

You may have come up with different suggestions. Mine are described below.

One light might be used to indicate that the camera is on. This might be flashing or steady. This would provide reassuring feedback, confirming that the camera is working correctly. The light would need to be bright enough to be visible in normal sunlight. The colour and rate of flashing of the light are not important.

A second light could come on when the camera is ready to take a photograph. A steady light would be most appropriate here, to show that the camera has reached a certain state. In some cameras this happens when the button is half depressed and the automatic focus is locked in. The light could be green, indicating that the camera is ready to go (although the colour may not be perceived as being green by those who are red–green colour blind). It should not be too bright as it will need to be positioned near to the viewfinder, where the photographer's eye will be.

A gauge might be used to indicate the battery level. The gauge could be a series of blocks displayed on a small LCD screen on the top of the camera.

Review Question 3

This section has introduced four different types of output devices: screen, printer, loudspeaker and simple devices (such as dials, lights and buzzers). The nature of the output delivered by each of these varies in terms of its persistence, i.e. how long it lasts.

Compare the output from each of these devices with respect to its persistence. What implications does this have for design?

3.5 | Alternative approaches to output

As with input devices, there is research into alternatives to the existing forms of output device. The following are a few of the other important areas.

Head-up displays are used in some aircraft and some vehicles. The idea is to move up important information a user needs to see into their line of sight, so they don't have to keep looking down to the dashboard or cockpit control system. To do this, head-up displays (HUDs) project the image so it appears to float in mid-air, just in front of the windscreen. Now the user's eyes don't have to refocus to see gauges and indicators on a dashboard, and then refocus again to see the road ahead. Studies measuring performance for HUDs in cars have found the timing between looking at dash-mounted instruments and looking back on the traffic is about two seconds, whereas a head-up display in this configuration takes only 0.5 seconds. In the time it takes your eyes to refocus at highway speed, your vehicle travels several car lengths further down the road. Wildlife, another vehicle or a pedestrian could suddenly pop out in front of your vehicle, and keeping your eyes on the road allows you to react sooner. In situations like this, every fraction of a second counts. This is a form of augmented reality.

Augmented reality is one form of interaction paradigm. See Unit 1 of this block for more information on interaction paradigms.

A **head-mounted display** (HMD) is a helmet that contains one or more screens that are positioned in front of the eyes. These allow the users to feel much more part of the **virtual world** created by the software. Often these are programmed, so the view of the world changes when the user moves their head. HMDs are increasingly used in virtual reality systems. There are also military uses for this technology. A HMD is illustrated in Figure 23.

Figure 23   A virtual reality headset

Stereoscopic displays create a three-dimensional effect by using two screens, one in front of each eye. The two images represent slightly different perspectives on the object and together they combine to create the illusion of three dimensions. These screens are usually found in a HMD. Box 5 describes a virtual reality system that uses a variety of unusual input and output devices, including stereoscopic displays.

Box 1: Training firefighters using virtual reality

In collaboration with the Atlanta Fire Department, Georgia Institute of Technology is developing a virtual reality system to train firefighters.

When directing the fighting of a real fire, a commanding officer will issue instructions to the other firefighters under his command to extinguish the fire. The *Firefighter Command Training Virtual Environment* simulates the incidence and events of a house fire. Through the use of a head-mounted display, or a computer screen, the commanding officer is able to view the virtual house fire. They can see the fire from different angles, and navigate the fire scene as the fire is in progress. Virtual smoke and flames are seen, as well as a team of animated firefighters who respond to the commanding officer's instructions. The environment will respond to the events for fighting a fire in a realistic way. For example, if a door is opened, which causes a gust of wind, then the smoke and fire will change accordingly. If a firefighter sprays water on a fire, then it should die down, but there would be more smoke created.

In the environment, if the correct sequence of commands has been issued, then the fire will be extinguished with the least amount of danger to the firefighting team, and minimal damage to the house.

Source: For more information, see St Julien and Shaw (2003).

4 Exploring interaction devices

Interaction devices are being developed all the time. The following computer activities will help you to explore the latest changes in interaction technology.

ACTIVITY
Computer Activity 1: Augmented reality

This activity will take approximately 45 minutes.

This activity provides you with the opportunity to explore some of the online resources relating to augmented reality and related technologies.

ACTIVITY
Computer Activity 2: Assistive technology

This activity will take approximately 45 minutes

This activity provides you with the opportunity to explore further two aspects of assistive technology: tactile diagrams and web accessibiity.

References

Baber, C. (1997) *Beyond the Desktop: Designing and using interaction devices*, Computers and People Series, London, Academic Press.

Partridge, C. (1999) 'Communication breakdown', *The Times*, 7 July 1999.

Preece, J., Rogers, Y. and Sharp, H.C. (2002) *Interaction Design: Beyond human–computer interaction*, John Wiley & Sons Inc, USA.

St Julien and Shaw (2003) 'Firefighter command training virtual environment', in Tapia, R., *Celebration of Diversity in Computing. Proceedings of the 2003 Conference on Diversity in Computing, Atlanta, GA*, pp. 30–33, and http://www.gvu.gatech.edu/gvu/virtual/fire/index.html [accessed 9 July 2004].

Tepper, A. (1993) 'Future assessment by metaphors', *Behaviour and Information Technology*, Vol. 12, pp. 336–45.

Unit learning outcomes

Having studied this unit, you should now be able to do the following:

LO7: Describe a variety of interaction devices. Throughout this unit you have encountered a large range of interaction devices.

LO8: Explain the significance of choosing the right interaction device. If you are unsure of this, then revisit Section 1.2 and Box 1.

LO9: Describe the difference between direct and indirect pointing devices and give examples of each. If you are unsure of the difference, then you should re-read the beginning of Section 2.2. If you are unsure of examples, then you will need to re-read the whole of Section 2.2.

LO10: Describe the difference between continuous and discrete interaction devices, and give examples of each. If you are unsure of the difference, then you should re-read the beginning of Sections 2.1 and 2.2. If you are unsure of examples, then you will need to re-read the whole of Sections 2.1 and 2.2.

LO11: Choose suitable interaction devices for a simple interactive product. The unit has provided some questions to ask in order to choose suitable interaction devices. These are spread throughout the unit. If you are unsure, try revisiting Activities 1, 2, 3 and 4.

These contribute to the course learning outcomes as illustrated below.

Linking the unit learning outcomes to the course learning outcomes

Unit learning outcomes	Course learning outcomes
LO7 and LO8	KS2: Communicate effectively to peers and specialists about requirements, design, and evaluation activities relating to interactive products.
LO9 and LO10	KU2: Define key terms in interaction design
LO11	KU7: Discuss accessibility issues for interactive products CS4: Produce a low-fidelity prototype for an interactive product based upon a simple list of interaction design principles

Comments on review questions

REVIEW QUESTION 1 ....

With the chord keypad, several keys are pressed at once in order to enter a single character. This kind of input device was used for deep sea divers who had restricted mobility (see page 208 of the Set Book).

A trackball is an inverted mouse. These are often used with games consoles.

REVIEW QUESTION 2 ....

Gesture represents continuous input as the system needs to monitor all movement to understand the gesture; iris and fingerprint recognition is discrete since it is essentially a picture of the iris or fingerprint; handwriting recognition and speech recognition are also examples of continuous input as both handwriting and speech recognition are continuous actions.

REVIEW QUESTION 3 ....

The output on a screen lasts as long as the screen is turned on and the window displaying the information has not been overwritten (on the screen). Output from a printer lasts much longer, but is also dependent on the kind of paper or other medium used.

Audio output is very transient unless it is recorded by another device, and disappears instantly it is heard. Output from simple devices also disappears instantly because these devices display output on a moment-by-moment basis.

The implication for design is that the persistence of the output should be taken into account when choosing output devices.

Unit 3: Understanding users

CONTENTS

Introduction to Unit 3

Block 2 considered the importance of investigating and capturing the characteristics of the product's users. One common feature of users is that they are all people, and hence they share some fundamental characteristics. In this unit we will look at what we can learn from the work of cognitive science, and hence we look at more general characteristics of people. Understanding some of the theory that underlies design guidelines will help you to see why some designs work well and others fail miserably. It will also help you to better understand the guidelines themselves and how to apply them.

This unit falls logically into two main parts. The first looks at the design implications of what we know about key cognitive processes (Sections 1 and 2). The second looks at how people cope with the demands of everyday life, and how these coping strategies can help us in designing successful interactive products (Sections 3 and 4).

The unit includes the following topics:

▶ Cognitive processes: attention, perception and recognition, memory, learning, reading, speaking, listening, problem-solving, planning, reasoning and decision-making

▶ Implications for interaction design of the main aspects of cognition

▶ Mental models

▶ Information processing

▶ External cognition.

In this unit, I will emphasise the first three topics listed above: cognitive processes, implications of cognitive processes for design, and mental models. Information processing and external cognition are important, but quite complex, concepts and so you only need to be able to define them.

IMPORTANT STUDY NOTE

You will find that there is a lot of jargon introduced in this unit, and you may also find the corresponding sections of the Set Book difficult to read and absorb. Rest assured that it is not important for you to remember all the terms that you will come across, although it is important to understand the concepts and their implications for interaction design.

What you need to study this unit

You will need the following course components:

▶ this book

▶ the Set Book

▶ the course DVD.

You will need your computer and Internet connection for some of the activities.

How to study this unit

This unit is based around Chapter 3 of the Set Book.

STUDY NOTE

I suggest that you divide your reading of Chapter 3 into two sections. First read Chapter 3 in the Set Book up to the end of Section 3.3. Then study Sections 1 and 2 of this unit.

Having completed this material, then return to the Set Book and read the remainder of the chapter before studying Sections 3 and 4 in this unit. You do not need to complete the Assignment on page 103 of the Set Book as I will be asking you to complete this later in this unit. However, you should read through the summary and key points of the chapter listed on pages 103–4 and check that you understand them.

As you read, use the Experience Record Sheet in the Appendix to write down examples of everyday things that you come across and that illustrate the ideas being described. For example, think about what happens when you are using a website with lots of animation on it. What happens to your attention? When you are using a microwave oven or a DVD player how often do you need to reach for the instruction manual to achieve your goal? You might find it helpful to photocopy the Record Sheet and have it by your side as you read the unit, and indeed keep it in your pocket for the week to jot down examples you come across in your daily activities, then use it to discuss these issues with fellow students or your tutor. You will also find an electronic copy on the course website.

1 What is cognition?

1.1 Review of the Set Book reading

> ### STUDY NOTE
>
> This section complements and extends Sections 3.1 and 3.2 of the Set Book. If you have not already read these sections of the Set Book, then I suggest that you do so before reading any further.

Section 3.2 defines cognition as 'what goes on in our heads when we carry out our everyday activities', and introduces a set of cognitive processes that are relevant to interaction design:

- attention
- perception and recognition. (Note, however, that the discussion focuses mainly on perception of information rather than recognition.)
- memory
- learning
- reading, speaking and listening
- problem-solving, planning, reasoning and decision-making.

The way these cognitive processes work has implications for how to design interactive products so that they meet usability and user experience goals. Examples of design implications that arise from understanding these cognitive processes are included in the boxes on pages 77 to 89 of the Set Book.

Being able to explain the implications of these cognitive processes for interaction design will help you to understand the impact of design decisions on the users and their experience. It will also help you to apply guidelines that are based on what we know about these processes more appropriately.

Review Question 1

Cognition refers to what goes on in our heads. The Set Book introduces six cognitive processes that have implications for interaction design, but there are many other things going on inside our heads. Suggest some other processes that would be covered by this definition of cognition.

Review Question 2

For each of the following design decisions, identify the cognitive process that is affected by the decision, and use your understanding of this process to explain why the decision has been made:

▶ including animated adverts on a web page

▶ the magnifying glass in acrobat reader

▶ structuring commands in a desktop application around menus

▶ greying-out commands that are not accessible or not relevant to the current operation

▶ including tactile feedback in a computer game control console.

Thinking about these issues may suggest examples of your own experience that you could document in your Experience Record Sheet (see the Appendix).

Review Question 3

Suggest some design decisions from applications you commonly use which reflect knowledge about the following cognitive processes:

▶ perception

▶ attention

▶ memory

▶ problem-solving, planning, reasoning and decision-making.

Review Question 4

It can be difficult to remember passages of a book that we have read passively. Why is this, and how can we ensure that we remember more of it? You may find it helpful to reflect on your experience of reading the Set Book.

The review questions above have asked you to reflect on some of your own experiences of interactive products. The following activity aims to deepen your understanding of the issues around cognitive processes and interaction design by asking you to identify examples of the application of this knowledge to an example website.

ACTIVITY

Computer Activity 1: Newspaper websites

This activity will take approximately one hour.

Newspaper websites can be very interesting to compare. They attempt to reflect the look and feel of the paper-based newspaper, but also to make the most of the electronic medium. Choose your favourite daily newspaper (e.g. http://www.independent.co.uk/, http://www.guardian.co.uk/, http://www.thesun.co.uk/) and consider the design of the front page. In particular, look at the design implications in the boxes on pages 77 to 89 in Chapter 3 of the Set Book and consider whether the design you've chosen to study takes account of this information or not. Explain your conclusions.

COMMENT

The front page I chose to look at was *The Guardian* for 20 October 2004 (from http://www.guardian.co.uk/), shown overleaf. I consider each set of implications for this page on page 75.

Figure 1   Home page for Guardian Unlimited of 20 October 2004

Attention: The only element of animation on this page was that the headline under the date was cycling through the main headlines for the day. The designers chose to use colour more than animation to capture attention. (Other newspapers I looked at had more animation.) My eye was drawn to the text highlighted in red before the other colours (salience). Note their use of other colours to signify different types of article. The page is quite cluttered. Red and black backgrounds only appear at the top of the page; blue is the main colour appearing on the rest of the page.

Perception: The colour of text is chosen to be different depending on the background colour used. This makes text legible and distinguishable from the background. Icons and sound are not used for this page.

Memory: This is not a particular issue with this web page.

Learning: The web page certainly encourages exploration. It provides summaries, headlines and titles for readers to become interested before exploring further.

Reading, speaking and listening: There is no sound output associated with this page. When the window is re-sized, the text remains the same size. There doesn't seem to be any way of increasing the type size (unless I use my own magnifier).

Problem-solving, planning, reasoning, decision-making: The headlines for each story appear on the page, but then you have to click on them to get the full story. The use of a headline and 'intro' text hides the detail of the story and allows the reader to decide whether or not to click to read the full story. In addition, knowledgeable users might decide to use the 'Go To' option at the top-right of the page in order to go to a certain section of the newspaper, e.g. world news, jobs, travel, and so on.

Although I have emphasised the importance of the design implications, and on the whole it is a good idea to follow the suggestions made, there are also occasions when designers will deliberately break the rules, and cause the user confusion or distraction. For example, some of the newspaper websites mentioned in Computer Activity 1 are quite busy and distracting. On page 274 of the Set Book there is another example of a crowded website. In this and other cases, the screens are cluttered because they reflect the style of the paper-based version in order to keep the brand consistent. You will sometimes find that there are several animations running on a website too, in order to advertise different products.

2 Applying knowledge from the physical world to the digital world

2.1 Review of the Set Book reading

Understanding users, their tasks and their context is important for interaction design. One aspect of this will be to study how members of the target user group currently perform their tasks. Having understood this, one design strategy is to emulate how users cope with everyday life in the physical world with comparable mechanisms in the digital world. There are advantages and disadvantages of taking this approach, but provided these are understood then this approach can be very powerful.

The key to deciding whether or not to emulate physical world strategies in the digital world lies in understanding the problem to be addressed and the strategies people have developed for coping with it in the physical world.

Review Question 5

What are the main disadvantages of emulating strategies from the physical world in the digital world?

Review Question 6

How is the idea of emulating physical world strategies in the digital world related to the use of interface metaphors?

Interface metaphors were introduced in Unit 1 and will be returned to again in more detail in Unit 4.

The following activity builds on Computer Activity 1, and asks you to compare the physical manifestation of a newspaper with its digital version.

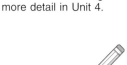

ACTIVITY 1

Consider again the newspaper website that you studied in Computer Activity 1. If you know the paper-based version of the newspaper, compare the two designs and see how much of the physical world has been translated into the digital world. What kind of changes have been made between the two?

COMMENT

The following is based on the Guardian website at www.guardian.co.uk considered in Computer Activity 1. You may have found other changes.

The paper-based version of the newspaper appears in Figure 2.

In search of the real artist
Turner prize review in G2

Jonathan Freedland
The US is in the middle of a religious revolution
Page 23

Five years in jail for being drunk and disorderly?
In Society **Plus** social care supplement

60p
Wednesday
October 20 2004
Published in London and Manchester
guardian.co.uk
* * *

The Guardian

British aid worker held in Iraq

Kidnappers release video footage of woman who opposed war

Jamie Wilson and **Patrick Barkham**

A British woman who has devoted most of her life to caring for the people of Iraq became the latest victim of Baghdad's ruthless kidnap gangs yesterday.

Video footage of Margaret Hassan, looking tired and drawn with her hands tied behind her back, was shown on an Arabic television channel. The Iraqi director of the charity Care International, 52, was kidnapped at around 7.30am on her way to work in the Khadra district of western Baghdad.

Her capture comes two weeks after the murder of Ken Bigley, the Liverpool engineer who was kidnapped in Baghdad and beheaded by Tawhid and Jihad, the militants led by the Jordanian extremist Abu Musab al-Zarqawi.

Wearing a cream shirt, Ms Hassan was shown on the video apparently talking, although no sound could be heard. The tape also showed Ms Hassan's identity papers and a credit card. Unlike most of the previous videos of kidnappings in Iraq, no militants or banners appeared.

It was not clear last night who had abducted Ms Hassan or why. Her husband told the television station al-Jazeera from Baghdad that his wife had been driving to work when she was kidnapped.

"When my wife was approaching her office, two cars surrounded her vehicle. The kidnappers attacked the driver and took control of her car, driving off with her to an unknown destination," Tahseen Ali Hassan said.

"We haven't heard anything about the group and no one has contacted us," he said.

The station said the footage of Ms Hassan was accompanied by a claim of responsibility from an unnamed Iraqi group. It was received "through the usual channels", a spokesman said.

Born in Dublin but married to an Iraqi and holding both Iraqi and British passports, Ms Hassan, who has lived in the country for more than 25 years, was a vociferous opponent of the sanctions that starved the Iraqi people of food, water and medical supplies after the war in 1991 and last year's invasion. Friends say she speaks Arabic with an Iraqi accent and considers herself Iraqi.

Care is one of the few charities still operating in Iraq after the abduction last month of two Italian aid workers. Both women were later freed after a ransom was paid.

Tony Blair said the government would do everything it could to secure Ms Hassan's release. "This is someone who has lived in Iraq for 30 years, someone who is immensely respected, someone who is doing her level best to help the country," he said. "It shows you the type of people we are up against, that they are prepared to kidnap somebody like this."

A spokesman for Care said in a statement: "As of now we are unaware of the motive for the abduction. As far as we know, Margaret is unharmed. Needless to say, we are doing whatever we can to secure her release."

Felicity Arbuthnot, an Irish freelance journalist who has known Ms Hassan for 15 years, said she was much-loved in Iraq: "She could go anywhere and didn't need a minder, even if she was going to a place that made Sadr city look like Knightsbridge."

Asked how her friend would deal with her captors, Ms Arbuthnot said: "She'll be talking to them in Arabic, keeping her voice calm and low and she will be talking and communicating. She's very used to people who feel very alienated, very hostile and very distant."

She said she hoped the prime minister would step back and allow the Irish government to lead the efforts to secure Ms Hassan's release.

'This is someone who has lived in Iraq for 30 years, doing her level best to help the country. It shows you the type of people we are up against'

The Foreign Office said the British embassy in Baghdad was in touch with Ms Hassan's next of kin.

The Irish foreign minister, Dermot Ahern, said his thoughts were with the Hassans: "I stand ready to contribute in any way we can to help secure her release."

Once again the kidnapping highlights the dangers for foreigners in Iraq. More than 140 have been kidnapped since April and dozens have been killed — none of them, however, foreign women.

Ms Hassan has worked tirelessly to improve the lives of ordinary Iraqis suffering from what she believed was a "manmade disaster" caused by a decade of sanctions and the war that finally toppled Saddam Hussein.

In the build-up to the war last year, she warned MPs of the humanitarian catastrophe another conflict would bring. In January 2003, she travelled to New York and spent a week briefing the members of the UN security council and UN agencies on the dire consequences of military action.

She heads an office of 60 Iraqi charity workers, and refused to leave her team during the war. They continued to work to give hospitals essential medical supplies, such as insulin, disinfectant and blood-testing kits, while also restoring sewage systems and access to clean water.

Ms Hassan embraced the ethos of Care, which prides itself on its policy of employing local staff. Ninety per cent of its 10,000 employees worldwide work in their home countries .

"We want to stress that she sees herself as an Iraqi," a spokeswoman for Care said. "Iraq is her home. She has been living there for many years and would never consider coming back to Britain."

Elsewhere in Iraq a mortar attack killed at least four Iraqi national guard soldiers and wounded 80 at a base north of Baghdad. An American contractor also died when mortar shells crashed into a US base in the Iraqi capital. And three car bombs exploded in the northern city of Mosul, killing two Iraqi civilians and wounding three.

Iraq crisis, page 4
guardian.co.uk/iraq

Margaret Hassan, the Iraqi director of Care, on the video shown by al-Jazeera. The charity said she saw herself as an Iraqi

Cabinet gamble on 'Las Vegas' casinos

Nicholas Watt and **Sarah Hall**

The battle lines were drawn for a pre-election row over gambling yesterday when the government published a 203-page bill introducing the most sweeping reforms in a generation.

The Tories joined forces with religious groups to accuse the government of paving the way for Las Vegas-style casinos which would place vulnerable people at risk.

The gambling bill, which should be on the statute book before next year's general election, is the culmination of three years' work. Ministers say they have to reform the law because new technology has meant that vast areas of the gambling business, particularly on the internet, are largely unregulated.

Their argument that the measure will offer new protection to gamblers has suffered a major setback after newspapers launched a campaigns against the plans.

The opposition has taken particular exception to the proposal to set up to 40 "regional casinos". Tales have abounded of how American companies are offering millions of pounds to induce local councils to allow them to set up huge casinos.

John Whittingdale, the shadow culture secretary, accepted the need to update the law but said the legislation as it stood could increase problem gambling and damage the gaming industry. All sides agree that there will be one key beneficiary. Spending on gambling is expected to increase from £8.7bn a year to £12bn within five years, netting a small fortune for the Treasury.

Full reports, page 3
Polly Toynbee, page 24
Leader comment, page 25
Tim Dowling, G2

Ministers hope to delay troop decision

Patrick Wintour
Chief political correspondent

The all-out US assault on Falluja is likely to be delayed until after the American presidential elections, but Tony Blair may face a decision before then on whether British troops will provide a support role in the US sector, Whitehall sources said yesterday.

Ministers have been caught badly off balance by the widespread assumption that they were preparing to bolster the US military as a political demonstration of support for George Bush ahead of the November 2 poll.

Amid signs of a serious backbench revolt, ministers would like to defer a decision until after the US poll. They were last night holding talks with Labour backbenchers to forestall a full-scale rebellion, reassuring them the request had come from the military and was totally focused on ensuring credible nationwide elections in Iraq.

A delay in the US assault would make it easier for Mr Blair to sell any British move into the more dangerous zone south of Baghdad as purely part of the overriding imperative to improve security ahead of the January 31 poll.

The British military reconnaissance yesterday in the area south of Baghdad may emerge with specific recommendations within days, including a timetable for British troop movement north. Defence secretary Geoff Hoon said on Monday he expected a final recommendation by the middle of the week. There were hints yesterday the advice may take longer to assemble.

The government has ruled out a vote on shifting British troops, but the Liberal Democrats want to find a parliamentary vehicle to gauge MPs' opinion.

The foreign secretary, Jack Straw, said Britain was looking at the US request sympathetically. Speaking at a joint press conference with Kofi Annan, the UN secretary general, he stressed Britain was not planning to increase its overall troop strength in Iraq.

NATURE. POWERFUL STUFF
ORIGINAL SOURCE MINT SHOWER
Now available in bottles of Original Source shower gel. For a free bottle visit originalsource.co.uk

India finally ends reign of the bandit king

Randeep Ramesh
in New Delhi

India's bandit king died as he lived: in dense forests at the tip of a bullet.

For more than two decades, Koose Muniswamy Veerappan eluded hundreds of police officers devoted to nothing but his capture.

Wanted for the murder of 130 people and for butchering 2,000 elephants, Veerappan taunted state governments, striking defiant poses in combat fatigues with his muzzle-loading rifle and his luxuriant handlebar moustache.

While his profile had never been higher, his powers had faded. Life on the run had taken a heavy toll on the 57-year-old. An ageing brigand with asthma and a bad stomach, he had recently lost the sight of his left eye, reducing considerably his ability to pass unnoticed through the south Indian forest.

His condition had made it easy for undercover police to infiltrate Veerappan's gang and convince the criminal mastermind to take a ride to a rural hospital.

Inside the van lounged Veerappan and three of his closest associates. Just before midnight on Monday, on a deserted jungle road, dozens of policemen ambushed and killed the outlaw and his henchmen in a 20-minute shoot-out.

"He had already shaved off his moustache to conceal his identity. But we had lured him into a trap. We ordered him to surrender but he refused. It was a pukka operation," said Jyoti Prakash Mirgi, the chief of Karnataka's special task force, who co-directed operations with his counterpart in neighbouring Tamil Nadu.

Although Veerappan had a $1m bounty on his head, a figure almost unheard of in India, this amount is a fraction of the 1.5 billion rupees (£19m) state governments have spent since 1990 hunting for him.

Such is Veerappan's myth that hundreds of locals went to the local hospital to ask police to put his body on display.

The legend of the bandit king began 40 years ago when forest rangers beat up a short, wiry young boy for trying to sneak after ivory poachers. A few years later Veerappan shot his first elephant and joined a notorious hunter's gang. Before long he had taken over the operation, and he committed his first murder in 1969.

Despite this bloody beginning, Veerappan was notable for little more than his facial hair. To many officials he was just another small-time poacher holed up in the woods. It was only when ivory sales were banned in 1986 that Veerappan began to display the ruthlessness, cunning and financial acumen that set him apart from other criminals.

His remarkable escape from behind bars that year by killing four policemen and an unarmed forest official in their sleep alerted state governments to his cold-bloodedness.

By the late 1980s he had made a small fortune illegally cutting and smuggling sandalwood. Veerappan also dabbled in extortion, demanding monthly payments from the lime quarry owners in the hills overlooking his jungle lair.

This activity soon alarmed the southern Indian states of Karnataka and Tamil Nadu, which straddled Veerappan's domain. The 5ft 6in charismatic outlaw with an excellent shot became the target of forest rangers from both states.

▸ Page 2

Austin

WE SEE IT AS THE FIRST STEP TO THE BOOKER PRIZE

Hollinghurst wins Booker prize

Alan Hollinghurst won this year's Man Booker prize last night for his novel The Line of Beauty, scooping £50,000 for a tale of Tory politics and gay lust

Full report, page 5

9 770261 307033 43
CE ABFPRST

Figure 2 The paper-based version of The Guardian

On the whole, the look and feel of the paper-based design (Figure 2) is reflected in the digital design (Figure 1). For example, the same blue highlighting is used at the top, and there is very little colour otherwise, apart from in photographs. Both versions also have tables of contents, although they behave in different ways (the online version is hyperlinked to inside pages, while the physical version relies on page numbers and page-turning).

One aspect which is quite noticeable from the two front pages is that in the paper version the main stories appear on the front page; they may continue on an inside page, but the text of the story is immediately accessible on the front page. On the website, no detail of the stories appears on the front page, only the headline and a one-sentence summary of the story itself. This is an example where the designers have exploited the nature of the different media. Paper is a serial medium, whereas the digital medium is more flexible. This means, for example, that headlines for all the stories can appear on the front page of the online version (in a priority order), whereas this would not be sensible for the paper version.

In summary, the digital version is not a straight copy of the physical paper that has just been copied across into an electronic form. The designers have been careful to make the most of the different media in each case.

Interestingly, the Guardian Unlimited home page has a link 'Read today's paper' which goes to a web page titled 'Today's stories' where a different style is portrayed. Here, there is a picture of the front page of the physical newspaper and more direct links to the stories (see Figure 3). There is also a digital version of the newspaper that can be accessed (for a fee).

Figure 3   The web page for 'Today's stories' in Guardian Unlimited

When you next look at your favourite ecommerce store, online newspaper, society page or whatever, spend a few minutes considering whether and how the site takes account of the cognitive processes you have learned about in this unit, and consider whether or how knowledge from the physical world has been translated into the digital medium.

Document these thoughts in your Experience Record Sheet.

STUDY NOTE

Now read Sections 3.4 and 3.5 of the Set Book.

3 Conceptual frameworks for cognition

3.1 Review of the Set Book reading

Section 3.4 of the Set Book presents three frameworks for cognition which are useful for interaction design. These are: mental models, information processing and external cognition.

A **mental model** is a mental construct within the head of the user which consists of knowledge of how to use something and knowledge of how it works. A user's mental model helps him understand and predict the behaviour of a product. So if a user develops an appropriate mental model, then this can make it much easier for him to achieve his goals when using the product. As an interaction designer, you cannot inspect a user's mental model, and you cannot build the mental model for a user. However, it is possible, for example through the use of suitable metaphors, and maintaining consistency through families of applications, to help users construct an appropriate mental model. Ideally, the mental model would map clearly onto the designer's conceptual model.

Information processing is one model of how the mind works that focuses on information entering and exiting the mind through a series of information processing steps. One application of this model has been to assign times to each of the information processing steps, and then to calculate how long it would take to achieve a specific task using a certain interactive product. This can then form the basis of comparison between different products. However it has been argued that the information processing model does not adequately reflect cognitive activity as it takes place in an everyday environment.

As opposed to the information processing approach, **external cognition** recognises that cognitive activity is influenced by elements from the external environment. In particular, external cognition emphasises the role that external representations take in our cognitive activities. The Set Book introduces three cognitive benefits of using different representations for cognitive activity:

▶ Externalising information reduces memory load.

▶ Using a tool to perform computations reduces the cognitive load.

▶ Annotating and modifying external representations as situations change makes it easy to view the current situation.

Of these three approaches, the mental model is the one we will focus on in this unit. The others are just as significant in interaction design, but they are also more complex. The user's mental model is a key consideration in interaction design.

Review Question 7

What are the two kinds of knowledge in a user's mental model?

Review Question 8

How can interface metaphors help a user to develop an appropriate mental model of a product?

Review Question 9

What is the main criticism of the information processing model?

Review Question 10

State one general principle for interaction design that is based on external cognition.

As the M364 course team view the mental model as being crucial to interaction design, I explain it further below. In Section 3.3 I then refer to the concepts of designer's model, user's model and system image, which you will originally have read about on page 54 of the Set Book. These concepts have an important relationship to the user's mental model.

3.2 Mental models

The idea of a mental model is not specific to software-based interactive products, and indeed we form mental models for all sorts of things in our everyday life. In the Set Book, you saw some examples concerned with heating and ovens. It is quite likely that you also have a mental model of a car engine, or how to fix the problem when your lawnmower stops working, and so on. Mental models are usually developed over time, and are organic rather than well-formed from the outset.

In the field of interaction design, it is common for reference to be made to the mental model of a complete system or product, but there are mental models associated with sections of a system or product too. For example, consider an email system such as Outlook Express. This has an address book where I can enter my personal contacts and a central phone list for my organisation. When I enter a name in the 'To' field of a new email message, the system automatically suggests names (and email addresses) from my address book that match my typing. Based on this experience, my mental model of an address book when it's part of an emailing system is that it will recognise names that I put into the 'To' field of an email, and automatically replace the name with the corresponding email address in my address book. Now when I go to a different email system, such as Yahoo mail, I assume that the address book will behave in the same way there as well, but it doesn't. I have to modify my mental model and take on board a different set of behaviours for the new mailing system.

ACTIVITY 2

Do the assignment at the end of Chapter 3 on page 103 of the Set Book. This asks you to write down your own mental model and to reflect on how you think an ATM works, and then to elicit mental models from other people and compare them with your own. To do this, you need to explain what you think the ATM is doing after you press each button. I suggest that you begin by considering the simple scenario of withdrawing some money, say £100. Then write a use case for this scenario (you met use cases in Section 4 of Block 2 Unit 2). The actions from the user are relatively straightforward, e.g. put card in relevant slot, choose the 'Withdraw cash with receipt' option, and so on. When you come to write the system responses, though, think carefully about what you assume the system is doing – e.g. when does it check your balance, when does it check the validity of the card, what background processing might it be doing, and so on.

Thinking about this may suggest experiences that you could document on your Experience Record Sheet.

COMMENT

When doing this exercise you will probably be surprised at just how little you know about how ATMs work (unless you have worked in a bank). One main reason for this is that, as far as you are concerned, an ATM is there to serve you efficiently and effectively. You just need to know how to operate it. It is only when unexpected things happen (e.g. it does not give you any money, it says you are overdrawn when you are not, it gives you more money than you asked for) that you may start to wonder how an ATM system works.

The answers you get for this activity will depend on the people from whom you elicit mental models, and how closely they match your own view.

(a) My use case looked like this (normal course only):

1   User pushes card into the slot on the ATM

2   System grabs card and pulls it into the reader

3   System checks card validity (i.e. is it a valid card for this ATM?)

4   System prompts user for PIN number

5   User enters PIN number

6   System checks PIN number is valid

7   System checks to see if card has been stolen

8   System displays the main menu of choices

9   User chooses the 'Withdraw cash with receipt' option

10   System displays the 'Withdraw cash' option screen for amount of money required

11   User chooses the £100 option

12   System checks amount requested against the card limit and bank account balance

13   System returns card

14 User takes card

15 System counts cash

16 System displays the reminder screen to wait for a receipt

17 System dispenses cash

18 System deducts £100 from bank balance

19 User takes cash (and puts it away)

20 System prints receipt and dispenses it

21 System re-displays Welcome screen.

There is no 'right' or 'wrong' answer here and your use case may have been (very) different. Having explored how you think the ATM works, it should have been easier to reflect on your model to answer the list of questions. Some of them are difficult to answer. For example, what information is on your card? All you can see is a magnetic strip on the back of the card. You have never been told what is written on it. You have to infer from your knowledge of banking what might be on it: maybe your pin number or account number? Your card limit? What else?

(b) What did you find when you asked other people? You may have discovered that their explanations were quite different from yours. It is quite common for there to be variability between people's explanations of the same system, but there are also different styles of ATM which interact in subtly different ways. You also may have found that people used incorrect analogies, superstition and bizarre models to explain their understanding. People can be quite creative when forced to provide explanations when they have no idea!

(c) One aspect of different ATMs I use is how the system reacts to data being entered. It is a small thing, but one which can cause user error and frustration. The ATM for my main bank insists that I press the 'Enter' key after input, while the ATM for a second bank I use does not. In the former case I have time to correct any error I've made before the system moves on, but in the latter I don't. I would much prefer the time to make changes and correct errors that the first model gives.

When ATMs were first introduced, different conceptual models were used by the different banks in the design of their ATMs. A key aspect was whether to (i) let the person take their money first and then give their card back or (ii) give their card back before letting them take their money. Banks that designed their ATMs on the first model found that a surprisingly high number of people forgot to take their card once they had achieved their primary goal of obtaining their cash. Conversely, banks that designed their machines using the second model didn't experience such problems. People rarely left their cash behind once they had removed their card! From an engineering perspective, the order in which they are performed may be regarded as arbitrary (so long as they are both executed). From an interaction design perspective, it is obvious as to why the order in which they are carried out by the user is crucial. Most ATMs nowadays adopt the second model.

(d) Having a clear conceptual model can help users create a more useful mental model of the system. For example, the conceptual model could be based on the kind of interaction a user will be more familiar with, such as dealing with a sales assistant. Alternatively, the ATM could indicate what is happening via images on the screen.

3.3 Design model, system image and user's model

You might find it helpful to re-read Box 2.3 on page 54 of the Set Book before reading this section.

The relationship between the user's mental model, the designer's conceptual model of the system, and the system itself is illustrated in Box 2.3 in the Set Book (page 54). This image shows that the design model (the conceptual model of the product as developed by the designer) is communicated to the user for him to construct his user's model (or mental model) via the system image (how the system actually works).

Here I expand on these ideas and explain how the design of a product can help the user construct an accurate mental model.

3.3.1 Design model

The design model is a more detailed version of the conceptual model that we discussed in Unit 1. It is therefore an explicit and consciously developed model, while the user's model (the mental model) evolves over time. For example, the design model of a car would include comprehensive knowledge of the way the engine, brakes, steering and other parts operate, knowledge of the design of other cars and knowledge of how to drive a car. The user's model, on the other hand, will be specific to the goals of the user. For example, if the user wanted to change the tyres, then her model will include details of how to jack up the car, remove the wheel, and so on; alternatively if the user wants to drive the car, then her model would involve information about how the gear stick, accelerator pedal, brakes and steering wheel can be used to drive. The design model is therefore typically not the same as the user's model, as it contains much more detail than the user would normally require. The system image for the car would include the various dials, knobs, lights, pedals, nuts, icons, manuals, tools, etc. which make up the interface to the car. Which elements of the system image are engaged with will depend on what the user wants to achieve.

The requirements activity of the lifecycle is important to the development of the design model. It is while undertaking this that the designer meets the users, observes them and talks to them, and hence gains an understanding of their goals and their perspectives. The interaction designer aims to communicate his own understanding of how the product works (the design model) through the working system. If he does this well, it should enable users to develop an accurate mental model, which will then enable them to achieve their goals more easily.

3.3.2 System image

The system image is the means by which the functionality and state of a system is presented to the user, and this can be through a variety of channels – through the interface, through training, through documentation including instruction manuals, and through online help.

The users acquire their knowledge of the system from the system image. The most important part of the system image is the interface since, through interaction with it, users build up their own mental model of the system and how it works. Users do not always read instruction documents, use the help function or receive training. Therefore, the maximum burden of influencing the user's mental model is on the interface.

Norman and Draper (1986) say:

> ... in many ways, the primary task of the designer is to construct an appropriate System Image, realising that everything the user interacts with helps to form that image: the physical knobs, dials, keyboards, and displays, and the documentation, including instruction manuals, help facilities, text input and output, and error messages.

They go on to discuss the implications for the system designer:

> If one hopes for the user to understand the system, to use it properly, and to enjoy using it, then it is up to the designer to make the system image explicit, intelligible, and consistent. And this goes for everything associated with the system.

ACTIVITY 3

Choose an interactive product that you use either at home or at your workplace. List the constituents of its system image.

COMMENT

I chose to consider an iPod music player (Figure 4), but you may have looked at a mobile phone, website or any other interactive product you know well. The system image of the iPod comprises the following:

Thinking about these issues may suggest experiences that you could document in your Experience Record Sheet.

▶ written instructions (a manual) that I received when I bought the device

▶ the scroll wheel on the front of the device

▶ the visual markings on this wheel

▶ the LED screen which displays various information about the device's state

▶ the online help available from Apple MacLink

▶ the headphones that produce sound when the device is on and is playing.

Figure 4   The Apple iPod music player

As designers, we are trying to create the system image in a way that accurately reflects our design model and so that the user's model will help them to understand the interactive product. One useful way of helping the users is for the system to have an appropriate interface metaphor.

3.3.3 User's model

When confronted with a new product, users often unconsciously 'run' their existing mental model to interpret the new situation, explain it and make predictions about the outcome of their interaction with the product. The mental model helps the users to answer questions such as 'What am I now seeing?', 'What did the system just do?', 'What have I done to make it do that?' and 'What should I do next?'.

The user's mental model of a new system will be based upon two things:

1   Existing mental models of systems, devices, tasks and other experiences that she sees as relevant to the new product. The users will have expectations of the new product based on these experiences, and if these are not met they may experience difficulties.

2   The system image for the new product. This should be designed to communicate effectively the relevant parts of the design model, in particular how the users need to operate the product in order to achieve their goals.

ACTIVITY 4

Consider the process of buying a train ticket from a railway clerk. You probably have a mental model of this process. How would this mental model help you purchase a ticket from an automatic ticket machine?

COMMENT

Your mental model probably includes telling the clerk where you are going, specifying the type of fare (single, return, off peak, etc.), and paying. You probably then expect the clerk to give you the ticket and a receipt. Therefore, in your head, you know what is involved in buying a ticket. You have a mental model of the process.

Suppose you want to buy a train ticket from a self-service ticket machine. From your original mental model, you probably know what you must do to get the ticket. You might anticipate the following: pressing various buttons to enter the information that you would have said to the railway clerk; inserting the money or a credit card into a slot; taking the ticket and receipt from other slots in the machine. In this way you are able to apply your 'old' mental model of buying a ticket from a railway clerk to this situation of interacting with a machine.

So when users interact with a new product, they apply their 'old' mental models and expect the new system to work in a way that their mental models suggest. For this reason it is important to take into account the users' prior knowledge and experience when designing a new interactive product. Users may become uncertain if their existing mental models do not explain how to use a new product (unless they can develop a new model quickly). They may proceed hesitantly and become frustrated, perhaps abandoning the new system entirely because it is unfamiliar.

Informing design: from theory to practice

4.1 Review of the Set Book reading

> **STUDY NOTE**
>
> This section complements Section 3.5 in the Set Book. If you have not already read Section 3.5 of the Set Book, then I suggest that you do so before reading any further.

Earlier in this unit, you read about design implications of various aspects of cognition. In Section 3.5 of the Set Book, other design tools which have been developed from cognitive theories, frameworks and models were briefly introduced.

For example the GOMS method was developed from the information processing model. This is a detailed task analysis approach to estimating the time it takes to complete a task. Another example is 'cognitive dimensions'.

You will find more detail of some of these in other units of the course. For example, specific design guidelines will be introduced in the next unit; evaluation methods will be introduced in Block 4.

Review Question 11

Miller's magical number 7 plus or minus 2 has been applied by designers in inappropriate ways (see Box 3.1 in the Set Book). Suggest a design guideline based on Miller's findings that would accurately represent them.

Reference

Norman, D.A. and Draper, S.W. (1986) *User Centered System Design: New perspectives on human–computer interaction*, Mahwah, NJ, Lawrence Erlbaum.

Unit learning outcomes

Having studied this unit, you should be able to:

LO12: Explain what cognition is and why it is important for interaction design. This was discussed in Section 1 of the unit. If you are unsure about this, then look again at Section 1 and Review Question 1.

LO13: Describe the cognitive processes of attention, perception and recognition, memory, learning, reading, speaking and listening, and problem-solving, planning, reasoning and decision-making. If you are unsure about this, then look again at Review Questions 2, 3 and 4.

LO14: Discuss, justify and apply a set of design implications that arise from the cognitive processes in LO13. These are presented in boxes on pages 77 to 89 of the Set Book. If you are unsure about these, then re-read these boxes and revisit Computer Activity 1.

LO15: Explain what a mental model is, and its significance to interaction design. This is described on pages 92 to 94 in the Set Book, and expanded in Section 3.2 and 3.3 of this unit. If you are unsure, then look again at Activity 4.

LO16: Define information processing and external cognition as frameworks for cognition. These are described on pages 96 to 101 of the Set Book. If you are still unsure about these, then look at the definitions in the Glossary, and on pages 96 and 98 of the Set Book.

LO17: Describe the user's model, design model and system image, and the relationships between them. If you are unsure of this, then revisit Box 2.3 on page 54 of the Set Book, and Section 3.3 of this unit.

LO18: Elicit a mental model and be able to understand what it means. If you are unsure about being able to do this, look again at Activity 2.

Linking the unit learning outcomes to the course learning outcomes

Unit learning outcomes	Course learning outcomes
LO12, LO15, LO16 and LO17	KU2: Define key terms used in interaction design
LO12	KU1: Explain why it is important to design interactive products that are usable
LO13, LO14 and LO17	KU6: Discuss theoretical or empirical evidence supporting a list of interaction design principles
LO18	CS1: Evaluate an interactive product using suitable techniques
LO15 and LO17	KS2: Communicate effectively to peers and specialists about requirements, design, and evaluation activities relating to interactive products.

Comments on review questions

REVIEW QUESTION 1 ....

Other processes I thought of include awareness, sensing, judgement, intellect and imagination.

REVIEW QUESTION 2 ....

- ▶ Moving images attract our attention more than static text. Advertisers want their adverts to be read, and so they animate their adverts. The cognitive process concerned is attention.

- ▶ The magnifying glass allows you to see the overall view of the document, yet also to magnify specific areas to be seen in more detail. The cognitive process concerned is reading.

- ▶ Using menu structures promotes recognition rather than recall. The cognitive process concerned is memory.

- ▶ If commands are greyed-out when they are not appropriate then the user will get used to which commands are appropriate when. The cognitive process concerned is learning.

- ▶ If the console shakes as though driving over rough ground at the same time that the game screen shows an image of driving down a rough road, then this increases your experience of the situation. The cognitive process concerned is perception.

REVIEW QUESTION 3 ....

I thought of the following examples, but you may have others:

- ▶ Picture-based menus on a mobile phone is an example of design informed by knowledge about perception.

- ▶ Using colour to highlight important information on a news website or a travel website is an example of design informed by knowledge about attention. Depending on the colour, or the 'logo', it could also relate to recognition.

- ▶ The feature in many internet browsers to complete a URL when you enter the first few characters is an example of design informed by knowledge of memory. It is also to help the user be more efficient by requiring them to type less.

- ▶ Providing hyperlinked explanations or definitions of terms within other documents, e.g. in Microsoft Help function, is an example of design informed by knowledge about problem-solving, planning, reasoning and decision-making.

REVIEW QUESTION 4 ....

The more attention that is paid to information, the more easily it is remembered. The degree to which we remember information is related to the degree to which the information has been encoded. We can improve our memory of information by reflecting on it, comparing it to other knowledge or experience we have, talking with colleagues about it, writing about it and so on. This is why it is important to complete the review questions and activities in this course.

REVIEW QUESTION 5 ....

When strategies from the physical world are translated into the digital world too literally they may over-constrain the user, or fail to make the most of digital possibilities.

REVIEW QUESTION 6 ....

The use of interface metaphors was discussed in Unit 1 of this block. Metaphors are used in order to help users understand new concepts by building on familiar knowledge. This usually entails taking experience from the real world and translating it somehow into the digital world. Emulating strategies from the physical world is one way of developing metaphors.

REVIEW QUESTION 7 ....

Knowledge of how to use the system and knowledge of how the system works .

REVIEW QUESTION 8 ....

The user will construct a mental model of the system based on their understanding of the metaphor being used. If the metaphor is appropriate then this will help the user construct an appropriate mental model.

REVIEW QUESTION 9 ....

The main criticism of the information processing view of cognition is that it focuses on the individual, without taking into account our interactions with external representations. The investigations on which the theory is built are regarded as rather artificial, ignoring the real-world context.

REVIEW QUESTION 10 ....

Provide external representations at the interface that reduce memory load and facilitate computational offloading, i.e. offer the user tools to help them carry out a computation.

REVIEW QUESTION 11 ....

A design guideline based on Miller's findings might be 'Do not expect users to remember more than five items at a time'. Of course, better interaction design would not require users to remember items at all if it could be avoided. Recognition rather than recall is another common design principle that insists that users are asked to remember as little as possible.

Appendix: Experience Record Sheet

This sheet is designed to be used alongside your reading of this unit to relate the ideas being presented to your own everyday experience. As you read, use this sheet to write down examples of everyday things that you come across and that illustrate the ideas being described. You might find it helpful to photocopy this page and have it by your side as you read the unit, and indeed in your pocket for the week to jot down examples you come across in your daily activities, then use it to discuss these issues with fellow students or your tutor.

You can also download an electronic copy of this sheet from the course website.

Concept or idea	Good examples from your own experience	Poor examples from your own experience
Design implications regarding **attention**, i.e. being directed to important information		
Design implications regarding **perception**, i.e. understanding information presented		
Design implications regarding **memory**, i.e. products relying on you to remember complex or opaque information		
Design implications regarding **learning**, i.e. where a product has helped or hindered your learning how to use it		
Design implications regarding **reading**, **speaking** or **listening**, e.g. speech systems that are difficult to understand		
Design implications regarding **problem-solving**, **planning**, **reasoning** and **decision-making**		
The use of **physical world ideas** in the digital world		
Mental models, i.e. your understanding of how a product works		

Unit 4: Design, prototyping and construction

CONTENTS

Introduction to Unit 4

This unit pulls together what you have learned in earlier units in order to produce a prototype. After introducing the different kinds of prototype that exist, the unit shows how conceptual design and physical design can be accomplished, using the concepts that you have learned in earlier units of this block, and also information from previous blocks. The unit shows you how to produce three kinds of prototype: storyboard, card-based prototype and interface sketch. The purpose of these different prototypes, and how they are related, is summarised in Figure 1. These prototypes may be constructed at any time within the product's development, and continue to evolve iteratively through (re)design and evaluation. Other forms of prototype can be and are built as part of interaction design, but we will focus on these three.

The unit has a fairly practical focus. My aim in this unit is to be more concrete about how to proceed with design.

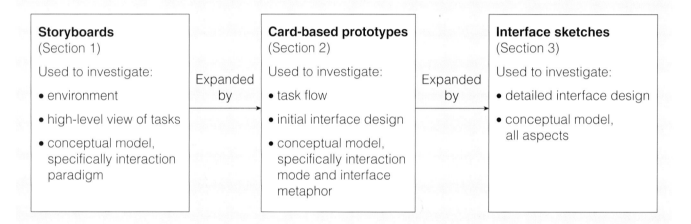

Figure 1   The three different prototypes introduced in this unit, and how they relate

The Set Book introduces you to many concepts in Chapter 8, backed up with examples and activities. However the aim of this unit is to provide you with sufficient knowledge and practical know-how to be able to produce a prototype. Hence this unit contains considerable extra material and more detailed guidance.

The unit will cover the following key concepts:

1   low-fidelity prototyping
2   high-fidelity prototyping
3   evolutionary versus throwaway prototyping
4   horizontal versus vertical prototyping

and will help you to be able to:

1   develop three kinds of low-fidelity prototype: a storyboard, a card-based prototype, and an interface sketch
2   identify and assess an interface metaphor
3   choose an appropriate interaction paradigm
4   develop and expand a conceptual model.

What you need to study this unit

You will need the following course components:

► this book

► Block 2

► the Set Book

► the course DVD.

You will need your computer and Internet connection for some of the activities.

How to study this unit

This unit is based around Chapter 8 of the Set Book, and the review questions, activities and extra material presented in this book.

STUDY NOTE

I suggest that you start by reading the whole of Chapter 8 of the Set Book, including the Boxes, and complete the Activities as you read, making notes or highlighting key sections. You do not need to complete the Assignment on page 277. However, you should read through the summary and key points of the chapter listed on page 277 and check that you understand them.

Then study the following additional material, readings, activities and review questions. These are organised in a similar way to Chapter 8 of the Set Book and are designed to both deepen and broaden your understanding of interaction design. Completing the activities will often require you to re-read sections of the Set Book, so they should help consolidate your understanding and mean you remember more when you come to revising.

Prototyping and construction

1.1 Review of the Set Book reading

Section 8.2 is quite a long section introducing the idea of **prototyping**: what it is, why do it, different types of prototyping, and some practical considerations when using prototypes. A prototype is a limited representation of a design that users and other stakeholders can interact with. Building a prototype may be done for a number of reasons, such as: to help during discussions with stakeholders, to support discussions among team members, to try out the feasibility of an idea, and so on. Producing a prototype helps designers to choose between alternatives. A user-centred approach to designing interactive products involves the production of prototypes at every stage of development.

The form a prototype can take is quite varied, on a spectrum from high-fidelity to low-fidelity. **High-fidelity prototypes** exhibit automatic interaction, have similar characteristics to the final product, and are usually built using a software environment such as VisualBasic. A **low-fidelity prototype** does not exhibit any (or only limited) automatic behaviour, does not look very much like the final product, and is built with other materials such as cardboard, paper and string. Prototyping in Microsoft PowerPoint is becoming more common too. A prototype in PowerPoint can be made to exhibit some limited interaction and has a 'look and feel' that is closer to the final product than paper would be.

There are two forms of paper prototyping introduced in the Set Book that I would particularly like to highlight: one is in the form of a storyboard showing the context of the interactive product and actions outside the design of the product itself (see Figure 8.2 on page 243 and Figure 8.4 on page 245 of the Set Book); and the other is a card-based prototype which is a set of sketches showing how the interface changes as the interaction proceeds (see Figure 8.9 on page 263 and Figure 8.10 on page 265 of the Set Book). We will also be looking briefly at more detailed aspects of interface design. Sketching is used in all of these approaches, and you don't need to be a great artist in order to get across your message. You can make up some easy symbols of your own to represent common items (but remember that others will need to understand them too).

In this section, I particularly stress the power of paper-based prototyping.

Review Question 1

What can a user gain from a prototype?

Review Question 2

A prototype may be high-fidelity or low-fidelity. Which type would you use for each of the following:

(a) to test whether the new system will be compatible with an existing wireless network?

(b) to clarify the flow of work documents between groups within the client company?

Review Question 3

Why do low-fidelity prototypes tend to be used early in development?

Review Question 4

In Table 8.1 (on page 246 of the Set Book) comparing high-fidelity and low-fidelity prototyping, one of the advantages listed for low-fidelity prototyping is 'Address screen layout issues'. Why do you think this is a significant advantage of low-fidelity prototyping?

Review Question 5

Is it possible to produce a low-fidelity vertical prototype?

Review Question 6

Two approaches to prototyping are: evolutionary prototyping and throw-away prototyping. How do they differ, and what is the consequence of choosing one rather than the other for product development?

Review Question 7

Storyboards as described in the Set Book are useful for prototyping some aspects of a system, but not all. What aspects do you think this form of prototyping is useful for exploring?

It is quite common for newcomers to low-fidelity prototyping to be quite sceptical of their efficacy. In Section 1.2 below, I hope to provide sufficient evidence to convince you that using paper and pencils to develop a prototype early on in development can be a very powerful aid to designing a good interaction. In the rest of this section I will show you how to develop your own storyboard based on a scenario (such as the ones you would develop during the requirements activity discussed in Block 2).

1.2 The power of paper

Low-fidelity prototypes are usually made using paper, index cards, sticky notes, pens, and other common office products. The idea of producing such a prototype may sound ridiculous, frightening, liberating, rewarding or foolish, depending on your perspective. If you have a programming background, you will probably understand the importance of high-fidelity prototyping, but you may not appreciate the power of low-fidelity prototyping. Using low-fidelity prototypes can be very advantageous in interaction design. One example of their use is described in Box 1. One major difference between high-fidelity and low-fidelity prototyping is that in the latter you're designing, while in the former you're programming. When you're designing you need the freedom to generate and consider alternative designs, and high-fidelity prototyping environments often constrain design creativity.

Low-fidelity prototyping, on the other hand, gives a designer the flexibility and freedom to explore alternatives and play with ideas, without any constraints of technology and without getting sidetracked into technical issues. For programmers or those used to prototyping in a software environment such as VisualBasic, this may seem a waste of time – after all, there are perfectly good widgets and template screen layouts in VisualBasic to support most tasks. However, if you use a set of pre-defined widgets then you are immediately imposing a certain look and feel on the interface, and constraints on the kinds of interaction possible. With paper and card you can sketch anything you want without any limitations. And more importantly the designer can explore many different alternatives relatively quickly. Remember from Block 1 Unit 3 that exploring alternative designs is the key to getting a good design, so the more alternative designs that are explored, the higher is the chance that a good design will emerge at the end.

All prototypes are built to explore certain aspects of a design. Low-fidelity prototyping, and specifically paper-based prototyping, is useful for exploring the following aspects with users:

This list is based on one in Snyder (2003) p.259.

1 *Concepts and terminology.* Unfamiliar or misleading terminology can cause users considerable problems. These can be identified using a paper prototype.

2 *Navigation, work flow, task flow.* A paper prototype isn't constrained by the number of paths that have been programmed into the interface. Although you will probably have an expected path through the interface, a paper prototype will have no constraints, and so the user is free to follow their own path.

3 *Content.* The prototype should involve the real content as far as is possible.

4 *Documentation/help.* As with concepts and terminology, a paper prototype can identify confusing or inappropriate terms and phrases, which in turn will influence the documentation written.

5 *Requirements/functionality.* If you've missed a piece of functionality then a paper-based prototype should help you to identify this fact.

6 *Interface layout.* A designer needs to understand what should appear on a particular screen or interface and what is the relative importance of the elements. A paper prototype shows the information intended to appear at any point in the interaction, together with its layout, how information is divided across screens, etc. It is therefore easy to spot deficiencies in this area.

Review Question 8

Interaction design proceeds through a cycle of evaluation and design or redesign. All of the issues above are important, but which one(s) will have the most impact on redesign?

Box 1: Using paper prototypes to manage risk

A true story reported on the website of the US firm User Interface Engineering

There are no rewards in life for being the first one with the wrong answer. Imagine spending years building a product, only to learn that it missed the needs of its intended market. History is littered with the carcasses of failed products and the companies that built them – product development is indeed a risky business.

We're a consulting firm specializing in user interface design and usability issues, so our initial contact with new clients is usually when they realize their product is in trouble. Here's a typical scenario: We got a call from the marketing manager for a commercial software product. The first release of the product had been around for a year, but sales had been only mediocre. Although customers liked the functionality, they complained that the software was difficult to use (the manager admitted that even people within the company had trouble using it!). The manager was worried that these problems were going to hurt sales of the next release, and that support costs would escalate. To manage these risks, the company needed to do something differently.

The company had spent considerable time and money to produce their first release, just to learn that they hadn't quite gotten it right. In a sense, that first release was actually a 'prototype' for the next release, a prototype that had taken many, many developer-years to build. Because their market had become increasingly competitive, the company couldn't afford another so-so release. And they couldn't wait years or even months for that key feedback – they needed it before their beta test, which was only a few weeks away.

That's exactly what we helped them do. Using the techniques of paper prototyping and usability testing, we showed the team how to get quick feedback on their product before they had invested a lot of development effort. Total time required: about 6 days.

Techniques and approaches (including usability testing) to evaluate designs will be discussed in Block 4.

Day 1

We met with the entire development team. Like every other team we've ever worked with, these people already had a rich set of opinions (and sometimes, heated arguments!) about what was wrong with the interface and how to fix it. The trouble was, they had very little actual data on which problems were most critical to users or on which of the potential solutions (none of which had been implemented) were actually going to solve the problems. Without this data, there was a considerable risk that the team would implement the wrong solutions or even worse, remain ignorant of where the real problems lay.

The first thing we did with the team was to agree on a profile of their most important type of user and the most important things that those users did with the product. There was no time in the schedule to exhaustively test every aspect of the product, so we had to focus on the riskiest parts – the things that were going to make or break the next release of the product. In this case, the team members agreed that the biggest risk was that the product was so hard to use that it would make a negative impression on the technical buyer. As another example, in an insurance claims processing system, the biggest risk might be 'Will users accept the way we've re-engineered the work flow?' If the team doesn't know where the risks lie, that in itself is probably the biggest risk!

Days 2 and 3

We started looking for people who fit the user profile to bring in for the usability test sessions. Meanwhile, we showed the team how to construct a paper prototype of the product interface so we could get some data about those high-risk areas. Using common office supplies (markers, index cards, scissors, transparency film) the development team quickly sketched each element of the interface (screen, menu, error message) on a separate piece of paper.

We completed the prototype by the end of Day 3. It wasn't very neat – it had hand-written text, crooked lines and last-minute corrections – but it was good enough to show what the screens would look like.

Although the image quality is poor I have retained the prototype image as a genuine example. You will not be expected to repeat any of the details in this illustration.

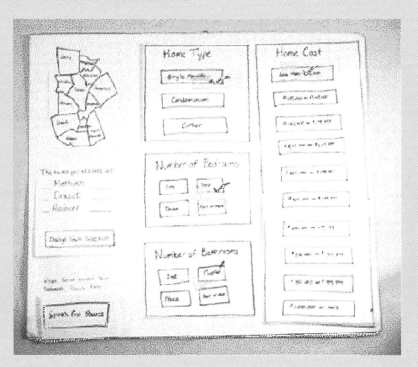

Days 4 and 5

We picked one developer to play the role of 'computer,' simulating the behaviour of the software by manipulating the pieces of paper. For example, if the user wanted to open a document in a Windows-based word processor, they would touch the word 'File' on the menu bar. The 'computer' would respond by putting down a piece of paper containing the File menu. The user would then touch the Open option, the computer would display the Open dialog box.

In paper-based prototyping, the 'computer' is the person who provides dynamic interaction by manipulating the interface elements to simulate how the final product is expected to behave.

We spent 2 days usability testing the paper prototype. In each test session, we brought in two people who matched the profile of a typical user. We didn't give them a demo or explain how to use the interface – instead, we asked them to do realistic work with the prototype. The computer wasn't allowed to explain anything to users, but could only do what the software was designed to do.

We didn't ask the users for their opinions of the interface; we watched them actually work with it (we've found that sometimes people say they love a product even though they can't use it, or vice versa). The entire development team observed the sessions, taking notes on where the interface was giving the users problems.

The team was surprised by many of the issues they saw. In some cases, we found that developers had been arguing about something that the users didn't even notice! At the same time, there were huge problems in the interface that no one had anticipated. Usability testing gave everyone on the team a sense of what the real issues were; the ones that would affect the success of the next release.

After each 2-hour test, the team discussed what they had seen and immediately made changes to the paper prototype. With a paper prototype, the entire team could collaborate on the design rather than funneling all the input into one or two programmers. Team members from all disciplines (engineering, marketing, technical communications, training and management) picked up the markers and scissors and contributed their expertise directly to the paper prototype.

Modifying a paper prototype is much less painful for the developers than modifying an actual product. With a real product, because of the substantial amount of work they've put in, the team has an emotional investment in the status quo and will naturally tend to 'defend' their design. Even when the team clearly understands the need for changes, it's tough to throw away all that hard work. In contrast, because paper prototypes are so easy to create and modify, there is less invested effort to defend. As a result, development teams become more flexible and willing to try new ideas. This team spent about 2 hours making changes.

After lunch, we brought in 2 different users and had them do the same tasks, to see whether we'd made the product better or worse. Most of the changes proved to be improvements. Some changes were as simple as using a different word, moving a button from the top of the screen to the bottom or putting an example in a help file. Other changes were more substantial – we've seen teams completely redesign their products, literally overnight, after learning that their current design was headed for disaster.

Day 6

After 2 days of testing, the team had identified and addressed many of the biggest problems in the interface. On Day 6, we again met with the entire team to prioritize all the issues that remained in the product, using data – not opinions – that we had obtained from the usability tests. Given their tight schedule (they were a month away from beta testing), the team knew where they had to focus their efforts in order to make the next release a success. On the seventh day, the team rested.

By using paper prototyping and usability testing, the development team managed their risks by focusing on them earlier in the project, while there was still time to make changes. We had started the process by having the team pick those areas which they had perceived as most critical to the success of the next release – the areas of highest risk. Now, 6 days later, they had actual data on how to make the product better in those areas. Our question for the team was 'OK, so now what's your next greatest risk?' The team now understood how to use paper prototyping and usability testing to provide the data they needed for key design decisions that enabled them to build a better product.

Review Question 9

In the story described in Box 1, users were asked to perform tasks with the paper prototype. Was there anything particular about the users or the tasks they were asked to perform?

1.3 How to develop a storyboard

Storyboards can be developed from the kind of scenarios produced during the requirements activity. The key strength of a storyboard is that it can show the context of use (environment) for the interactive product being developed. It can also be used to check out the interaction paradigm chosen for the product (see Section 2.4 below) and provide a high-level view of the tasks it supports.

Interaction paradigms were discussed in Unit 1.

The scenario for KitchenMade (presented in Block 2 Unit 2, Activity 14) is repeated below. You may remember that KitchenMade is intended to support elderly people in their own homes to choose and cook suitable meals according to diet and season. I want to show you how to produce a storyboard to represent this KitchenMade scenario. I will use the storyboards shown in Figures 8.2 (page 243) and 8.4 (page 245) of the Set Book as a template.

> Albert Sharples is a diabetic, which fact he has already entered in KitchenMade. One day, he feels no enthusiasm for cooking or for shopping, but turns on the KitchenMade and asks for suggestions for main meals which are suitable for diabetics, cheap, easy to cook and use seasonal ingredients. The system shows him enticing small video clips of possible meals, one of which really catches his fancy. He asks for a shopping list, which the system produces and he prints out. He checks his cupboards for ingredients, and then sets out for the shops with a spring in his step.

Review Question 10

In Unit 1 and on page 38 of the Set Book, there is a set of questions to help uncover assumptions that have been made implicitly when developing an idea for a product. However, assumptions can also creep in during the requirements activity when trying to develop concrete examples of use such as through scenarios. Read the KitchenMade scenario again, and identify any design decisions or assumptions about the interaction paradigm that are implicit within it.

As shown in Review Question 10, it is easy for assumptions and design decisions to be included within the requirements developed for a product. It is important to challenge and question all such assumptions during these early stages of design.

Essential use cases were introduced in Block 2 Unit 2.

To create a storyboard from a scenario you need to break the scenario into discrete steps that can be drawn as distinct actions within the storyboard sequence. This is similar to the process you might go through in order to develop an essential use case, and indeed an essential use case could also form the basis of a storyboard.

In this example, the scenario can be divided into four steps: Albert asks for suggestions from KitchenMade, Albert is offered some suggestions and chooses what he wants, the shopping list is printed, Albert goes off to the shops. These are represented in the storyboard in Figure 2, but in light of the answer to Review Question 10, I have avoided representing the system as a desktop PC. Note that there is not much detail in the sketches regarding the interaction between Albert and KitchenMade. If we wanted to prototype these, then we would develop a card-based prototype (described later, in Section 2).

(1) Albert asks for suggestions

(2) Albert is offered suggestions + chooses

(3) Shopping list is printed

(4) FOOD SHOP

Albert goes to the shop

Figure 2   Storyboard for KitchenMade

This storyboard captures activities beyond those performed directly with the interface of the interactive product, i.e. it considers the environmental requirements of the product. Also, note that the interactive product is drawn as a box, thereby deliberately leaving the interaction paradigm unspecified. If the system were drawn, say, as a keyboard and desktop computer then the exploration of the problem might miss significant alternatives.

Environmental requirements were introduced in Block 2 Unit 2. These requirements will have been captured for the product during the requirements activity.

Some applications will be less amenable to the use of storyboards. This does not mean that context is any less important for the system, but simply that it may be harder to represent the salient elements of the context in a storyboard. For example, consider the shared calendar example which is used in the Set Book. In particular, consider the scenario for this system on page 224. It would be possible to draw a storyboard to capture this kind of activity, but it would be very simple because all the activity takes place through the screen, and a storyboard would just include pictures of the user entering data into a system. Note, however, that thinking about context and the need to develop a storyboard might lead you to consider different interaction paradigms.

I have presented how to develop a storyboard from a scenario, but the scenario does not have to come first. Either could come first, or they could evolve together. A storyboard could equally well be developed in combination with an essential use case, or a use case.

ACTIVITY

Computer Activity 1: Creating a storyboard

This activity will take approximately 30 minutes.

This computer activity illustrates how the storyboard for KitchenMade was developed from the scenario, and the kind of issues the designer considered when drawing it.

ACTIVITY 1

In Activity 7.3 of the Set Book (Block 2 Unit 3), you were asked to develop a futuristic scenario for buying a new car.

(a) Return to the scenario you developed, and represent it as a storyboard. Remember that it does not need to be detailed or very pretty. The important factor is to consider the system and its context.

(b) Having drawn it, reflect on the process you went through, and what questions were in your mind as you sketched the interactions.

(c) The 'one-stop car shop' should be available to anyone who might want to drive a car; however, your storyboard may make assumptions about those users and their characteristics. Review your storyboard and identify any assumptions you have made.

COMMENT

(a) Looking at the scenario on page 226 of the Set Book, it is possible to divide it up into four chunks: Going to the one-stop car shop; Going into a booth; Inside the booth – choosing the car; Driving a simulation of chosen car. My storyboard is shown in Figure 3.

(b) I found that drawing the storyboard prompted me to think about the system and to consider questions such as: The scenario doesn't cover anything to do with using the printer, nor does it comment on any equipment required to experience the simulation, nor is it clear what happens to the keyboard once the simulation starts. Does there need to be a steering wheel? Gear stick? Pedals? You may have come up with other considerations and questions.

(c) The storyboard itself makes few assumptions, but the questions it raised in my mind led me to think about user controls, such as gear stick, pedals, etc. A disabled user would want different controls from a non-disabled user.

When developing a storyboard from a scenario, remember to question the assumptions that may be implicit within the expression of the scenario, and refer back to the environmental and user requirements of the product.

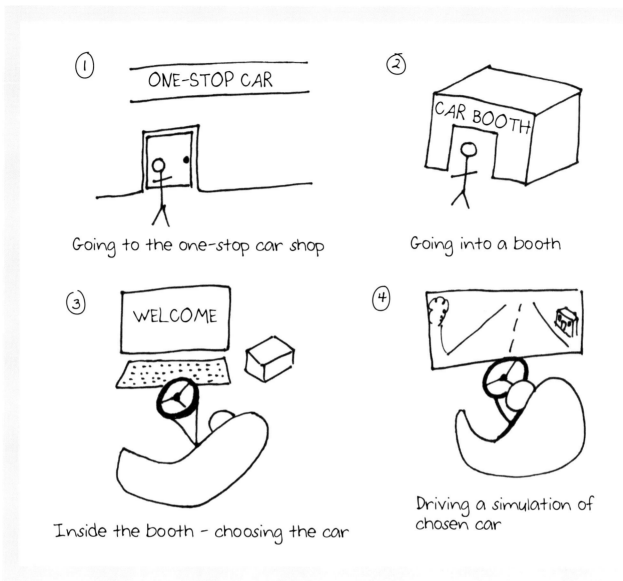

Figure 3   Storyboard for the one-stop car shop

Review Question 11

Storyboards and early prototyping are intended to focus on the conceptual design of a product. Based on your experience of drawing storyboards, suggest some disadvantages of this approach.

Remember that storyboarding and scenario building are iterative. The first version you produce will have faults, assumptions and misunderstandings embedded within it. Reflecting on your work, presenting it to others and discussing your ideas will help to uncover any problems.

ACTIVITY

Computer Activity 2: Reviewing a storyboard

This activity will take approximately 30 minutes.

This computer activity illustrates how a storyboard created by one designer can be reviewed by a colleague, and further issues identified.

2 Conceptual design: moving from requirements to first design

2.1 Review of the Set Book reading

The first step in moving from requirements to design is to explore the conceptual model. There is no right or wrong way to develop a conceptual model, but there are three implicit activities that are usually undertaken. Although they are presented in sequence, each may be iterated several times.

The *first activity* is to explore the problem space of the intended product. This process will have begun during the requirements stage, and will continue through problem space exploration as discussed in Unit 1 of this block. Activity 2 below asks you to apply these questions to the one-stop car shop.

The *second activity* is to consider different aspects of a conceptual model in order to envision what the product will be like. The aspects introduced in Unit 1 were: interaction mode, interface metaphor and interaction paradigm. Each of these provides a different perspective on the product and helps to understand its potential and limitations. Prototyping ideas helps to explore and evaluate the emerging design.

The *third activity* is to flesh out the initial ideas from the second activity by asking questions about the functions that the product will perform, how the functions are related to each other and what information needs to be available. Again, prototyping ideas will help to explore and evaluate the design. For example, a card-based prototype can be developed to illustrate and initially explore how the task is split across screens and some early interface design. A more detailed (possibly still low-fidelity) prototype would then be developed as a next step. This course does not cover the development of a full and detailed prototype.

These three activities and their relationships with different prototypes are summarised in Table 1.

Table 1　Three activities implicit in developing a conceptual model

Activity	Main purpose	Main evaluation vehicle
Explore problem space	Challenge assumptions about intended product	Requirements Storyboard prototype
Develop conceptual model	Identify interaction mode, paradigm and interface metaphor (if any)	Storyboard and card-based prototypes
Expand conceptual model	Add detail about the design.	Card-based prototypes and interface sketches

Each activity will involve iteration, reflection, considering alternatives, and production of prototypes. These prototypes then feed into the iterative cycle of design, evaluate and redesign, as the product evolves. Task descriptions such as scenarios, use cases, and essential use cases, task representations such as HTA diagrams, and any completed Volere shells, can be used to support this process together with prototypes (as introduced in the previous section).

Techniques for task description and task analysis were introduced in Block 2.

Underlying **conceptual design** there are four guiding principles (page 250):

1　Keep an open mind but never forget the users and their context.

2　Discuss ideas with other stakeholders as much as possible.

3　Use low-fidelity prototyping to get rapid feedback.

4　Iterate, iterate and iterate.

Probably the hardest aspect of these is to always challenge your assumptions and to listen to the results of evaluation. Having identified a suitable design for a system it can be difficult to then change direction and come up with different ideas. Considering the product from different stakeholder perspectives can help.

Details of evaluation will be addressed in Block 4.

Review Question 12

Box 8.2 in the Set Book describes experience prototyping. How can experience prototyping help to keep stakeholders' needs and the users' characteristics in the designers' minds?

Review Question 13

A conceptual model based on activities is more appropriate for a system that is designed to support a process, while a conceptual model based on objects is more appropriate for a system designed to support users in developing a specific product. Which model is most likely to be suitable for each of the following? (You may find it helpful to refer back to Unit 1 in this Block, and Chapter 2 in the Set Book.) Justify your choice.

(a)　a system to support a call centre handling customer queries in a bank

(b)　a touch-screen application to produce a collection ticket in a warehouse shopping outlet.

Review Question 14

How can plus and minus scenarios help in conceptual design?

Review Question 15

Scenarios can play a variety of roles: a basis for overall design, technical implementation, cooperation within the design team and as communication across professional boundaries. In Block 1 we discussed the perils and joys of working in a multidisciplinary team. Why do you think scenarios can help support this effort?

In the rest of this section, we will explore the three activities of conceptual model development, starting with Activity 2 which asks you to explore the problem space of an intended product.

ACTIVITY 2

In Block 3 Unit 1 (Chapter 2 page 38 of the Set Book) three sets of questions were introduced for understanding the problem space:

(a) Are there problems with an existing product? If so, what are they? Why do you think there are problems?

(b) Why do you think your proposed ideas might be useful? How do you envision people integrating your proposed design with how they currently do things in their everyday or working lives?

(c) How will your proposed design support people in their activities? In what way does it address an identified problem or extend current ways of doing things? Will it really help?

These questions are designed to uncover assumptions regarding a new product. Using these questions, explore the problem space of the project to develop an interactive system to support the purchase of a new car (building on your work for Activity 1 in the previous section).

COMMENT

The questions and my answers are given below. You may have arrived at different answers.

(a) *Are there problems with an existing product? If so, what are they? Why do you think there are problems?*

In this case, it isn't so much problems with an existing product as a desire to improve an existing situation. One of the disadvantages of the existing way to assess and buy a new car is that it is time-consuming and you may have to travel a long way or wait a considerable time before it would be possible to view the car of your choice.

(b) *Why do you think your proposed ideas might be useful? How do you envision people integrating your proposed design with how they currently do things in their everyday or working lives?*

The proposed ideas might be useful because it will bring a wider selection of new cars to the attention of potential car buyers. People might stroll down to their local one-stop car shop instead of browsing car showrooms. This increased choice might increase the likelihood of identifying a suitable vehicle. It might also breed discontent and frustration together with information overload. In addition, there doesn't seem to be a role for the car sales person in this, who would then be out of a job.

(c) *How will your proposed design support people in their activities? In what way does it address an identified problem or extend current ways of doing things? Will it really help?*

How the proposed system will support car buyers is illustrated in the scenario already. As indicated in the answer above, there are potential disadvantages to this kind of system in terms of how it will extend people's awareness of different vehicles on the market, and the likely effect on car sales staff. Whether the introduction of this system would have an overall positive or negative effect is a matter of ethics and opinion.

We will now consider in more detail the second and third activities in developing a conceptual model. The following material guides you through choosing an interaction mode, an interface metaphor and an interaction paradigm for a particular product. We then discuss expanding the conceptual model, and finally look at how to develop a card-based prototype. The third kind of prototype we cover, interface sketches, are covered in Section 3.

2.2 How to choose an interaction mode

Interaction mode refers to whether the conceptual model is based on an object or on activities. If the conceptual model is based on activities, then we will refer to the type of activity as being one of instructing, conversing, manipulating and navigating, or exploring and browsing (see Figure 4). **Interaction style** refers to the detail of how to instantiate a particular mode.

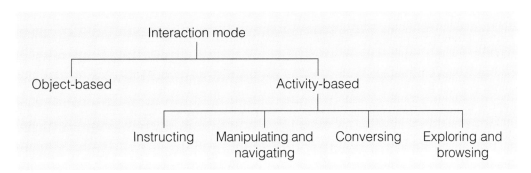

Figure 4   The interaction mode can be object-based or activity-based

The first decision to take regarding the interaction mode is to choose between an object-based mode or an activity-based mode. As mentioned in the Set Book, Mayhew gives a good distinction between these two basic types:

A product-oriented model will best fit an application in which there are clear, identifiable work products that users individually create, name and save.

A process-oriented model will best fit an application in which there are no clearly identifiable primary work products. In these applications, the main point is to support some work process.

Source: Mayhew (1999) p. 193

We will adopt these definitions for object-based mode and activity-based mode respectively.

Review Question 16

Is the conceptual model in the Tokairo case study introduced in Block 1 based on objects or activities? Justify your answer.

Sometimes it is not clear whether an interactive system is driven by a product or not, and it depends on the perspective you take. For example, consider a system to support the registration of membership details at a sports club, where every member is issued with a membership card. One perspective is to say that the system's main purpose is to support the process of registration, and hence an activity-based mode would be appropriate. However, an alternative perspective is to focus on the membership card and its production, and hence an object-based mode would be preferable. Being able to take different perspectives on the problem is nothing to worry about. This is why we spend time talking with users, and allow iteration, prototyping and redesign. If it is difficult to tell from the data you've collected during the requirements activity which of these perspectives is more appropriate, then the simple answer is to prototype both and let the users decide. The beauty of low-fidelity prototyping is that it is cheap, simple and quick to design and redesign again.

It is also common for one product to contain some aspects of an object-based nature, and some of an activity-based nature. For example, KitchenMade has two aspects: one object-based and the other activity-based. When the user first starts using the system, she will need to enter her own dietary requirements and preferences. This set of requirements is a 'clear, identifiable product', and hence this part of the system would best suit an object-based mode. The other aspect is to help choose a suitable recipe for the day. Note that the user is not creating the recipe, but choosing one, hence an activity-based mode (e.g. navigating and browsing or conversing) would be more appropriate for this aspect of the system.

ACTIVITY 3

Consider again the system to help users buy a new car. You produced a storyboard for this system in the previous section.

Which interaction mode would be most suitable for such a system? Give reasons for your choice. If you decide that an activity-based mode would be useful, then you should also choose the type of activity to be supported.

COMMENT

The main purpose of the one-stop car shop is for users 'to buy a new car' (from the scenario on page 226 of the Set Book). It is reasonable therefore to assume that at the end of the session a user wants to have a specification of the car they would like to buy. There is therefore a clear, identifiable product as output from the system. One design would therefore be structured around filling in every element of the specification, such as make, model, year, colour, additional features, and so on. Without prototyping this idea it is difficult to see how users would react, but there is a sense in which this kind of mode would not be in keeping with the intention of the product, which is more about experiencing different makes and models.

Driving a car is definitely activity-based, and there is no clear work product from this activity. Therefore at least some element of the system needs to support the activity of driving. The most suitable activity type for this would be manipulating and navigating as the user is driving in a virtual space, using their understanding of the physical world. (See page 47 of the Set Book for more information on manipulating and navigating.)

2.3 How to choose an interface metaphor

Three steps to choosing an **interface metaphor** are given on page 253 of the Set Book: understand what the system will do, understand which bits are likely to cause users problems and finally generate metaphors. These three steps may appear simple, but here we will look at them in more detail and I will provide some extra guidance about how to accomplish them. To do this, we consider the KitchenMade system introduced in Block 2 where some requirements were identified and a scenario was produced:

1   *Understand what the system will do.* This is achieved through the requirements activity, e.g. by generating scenarios such as the one you saw in Block 2. This system is to provide users with access to nutritious recipes, tailored to their specific circumstances. Understanding what users want is a central activity in interaction design.

2   *Understand which bits are likely to cause users problems.* In practice you would and should consult a set of users to answer this question, but from what we know about the users, interacting with the system might itself be daunting, and so the system needs to be unthreatening and as familiar as possible. There may also be some more detailed concerns that we would want to address with a familiar metaphor, but for the example here I will concentrate on making the system approachable.

3   *Generate metaphors.* The kinds of items the users are likely to be familiar with, and which are related to KitchenMade's purpose, include books (specifically cookery books), television, paper-based forms, and telephone. Of these, the cookery book and television fit closely with the intention of accessing recipes while the paper-based forms fit closely with tailoring the system to the user's own needs. It might even be useful to sell a set of paper forms with the system so that users can complete some information before using KitchenMade itself, if this helps.

Having identified some suitable metaphors for KitchenMade, we then need to assess their suitability. To do this we can use the five questions on pages 254–6 of the Set Book to see if they are suitable. But before this can be done, you have to analyse the metaphor and identify some of its key characteristics: what elements does it have, what can you do with it, and what can't you do with it (what are its limitations?). Remember, however, that we are viewing this physical entity as an interactive product, i.e. we are not interested in its internal workings, but its key interaction characteristics. For example, what makes a cookery book a cookery book?

Remember the importance of generating alternative designs. Each interface metaphor you consider could generate a different design.

▶   *What elements does a cookery book have?* This is a book and therefore has pages, a cover (probably), some kind of binding to hold the pages together, an index, and a table of contents. It contains recipes, and recipes are usually presented in a particular form, and although the form may vary, the basic structure usually includes: a list of ingredients, a set of steps for cooking the dish, and the oven temperature (if required). It would not be unusual for the recipe to include a picture, an estimate of preparation and cooking time, utensils required and the number of people for whom the amounts are sufficient.

▶   *What can you do with a cookery book?* With a book, you can carry it around, for example to the shops or between rooms in the house, you can open it and turn the pages, use the index to look for specific items, and the table of contents to access the material grouped under a set of headings.

▶   *What can't you do with a cookery book (i.e. what are its limitations)?* There are many things you can't do with a book, but in this context some key aspects are that you can't taste or smell the dish, you can't search (usually) to find a dish that is cooked at a particular temperature, or that doesn't need milk, you can't talk to it, and it doesn't talk to you.

ACTIVITY 4

Another potential metaphor for KitchenMade is the television. Use the same questions described above to identify some of the key interaction characteristics of a television: what elements does it have, what can you do with it and what can't you do with it?

COMMENT

You may have come up with different ideas. Here are my thoughts:

What elements does it have? A television is usually a box (it can be one of many different sizes) with a screen. There will be a set of buttons and/or knobs to press or turn. Most televisions include a remote control handset that replicates or maybe replaces the set of controls on the television itself. The television doesn't operate very well without some mechanism for receiving a signal, such as an aerial or cable connection. You can also connect the television to a DVD player or video player and watch your own choice of film or programme.

What can you do with it? With a television you can watch and listen to animated programmes and films broadcast via the receiving mechanism you have, such as cable, satellite, etc. You can change channels by pressing buttons or turning knobs on the television on or the remote control. If the television is enabled for Ceefax, then you can also receive static pages of information, and can have sub-titles for programmes that support this feature. If enabled, you can also access the internet and send email. Interactive television allows you to influence the outcome of a programme you are watching. You can also adjust the appearance of the picture and the sound, e.g. increasing contrast, changing the size and shape of the picture (within limits), etc.

What you can't do with it (i.e. what are its limitations?) You can't talk to a television (and have it understand you), you can't fast-forward the programmes you're watching unless they are pre-recorded. The main feature that you can control relates to which channel the television is tuned to, and of course whether it is on or not.

In Table 2 I have used the five questions on pages 254–6 of the Set Book for assessing a metaphor to consider the suitability of the cookery book and television as metaphors for KitchenMade.

Table 2   Comparison of the cookery book and television metaphors for KitchenMade

	Cookery book	Television
How much structure does the metaphor provide?	The book will have a table of contents and an index. The recipes are usually collected together in categories. Each recipe will have a particular structure.	The programmes are collected together in channels. You are able to swap between channels at will.
How much of the metaphor is relevant to the problem?	The content (recipes) and structure of the content are relevant.	The ability to show practical application of instructions is relevant. Use of colour and sub-titles is also relevant.
Is the interface metaphor easy to represent?	Yes	Yes
Will your audience understand the metaphor?	Yes	Yes
How extensible is the metaphor?	Videos and other animations/ sound etc. can be added in much the same way as a multimedia education tool can be designed to be much more than a simple textbook.	You can add more 'channels' but that's about all. It's not very extensible.

Neither of these metaphors is sufficient on its own, and so we would need to include others in order to complete the required functionality. For example, collecting information about the user is not an activity easily accommodated by either of these metaphors. Although both could be massaged to allow this kind of input, it would not help the users and it therefore would not be at all advantageous. The paper-based forms metaphor identified above may be better for this aspect of the system, but as with any potential metaphor it would need to be carefully assessed.

ACTIVITY 5

In a recent visit to a warden-assisted home for the elderly, as part of your investigations for the KitchenMade product, you discover that most of the people interviewed find that the practical demonstrations offered by television programmes on cooking are easier to follow than written instructions in a cookery book. This is because they can watch the programme and follow what is happening at the same time, whereas reading from a book causes interruption to the flow of activity and can be confusing. How would you use this information in developing your conceptual model?

COMMENT

One reaction to this might be to stop considering the use of the cookery book as a possible metaphor and to concentrate more on using videos or speech to communicate recipes. However, your information is based on only a small set of users (relative to the number you hope to attract to the product) and so dismissing other metaphors would be inappropriate at this point. It would be sensible for you to design the next prototype to include this kind of interaction and to demonstrate it to users.

2.4 How to choose an interaction paradigm

There is a lot of information on **interaction paradigms** in the Set Book and in Unit 1 of this block, so I am not going to provide you with any further explanation. We will instead discuss the KitchenMade example and consider how to choose a suitable interaction paradigm for this system.

Choosing a paradigm involves considering the alternatives available and assessing them in the context of the user requirements, usability goals, user experience goals and other requirements.

The interaction paradigms introduced in Unit 1 were: ubiquitous computing, pervasive computing, wearable computing, tangible bits, attentive environments and Workaday World. In the storyboard shown for KitchenMade in Figure 2 of this unit, the system is drawn as a plain box, and the shopping list is printed out on a piece of paper. This already assumes something of the interaction paradigm to be used, so we should take a step back from this and consider alternatives. If we consider different paradigms, then it is possible to imagine different situations. For example, the system could be a mobile device, maybe a wearable. This way, the user could carry the device with them to the shop and then there may be no need for a shopping list to be printed – the device could 'speak the list' to the user once they were there.

Considering a ubiquitous approach we might envision the system becoming transparent to the user, and maybe incorporated into the common items in the user's kitchen such as the cookery book, or fridge-based shopping list. In this scenario the system would work quietly behind the scenes and might suggest options without the user needing to explicitly ask. Taking the idea further, we could also envisage a paradigm where the information and functionality are available at the local shop, so there is no need to carry anything to do the shopping. But then, with a smart fridge the system could do the whole lot from checking which ingredients are available to ordering the necessary provisions and getting them delivered.

While this may sound attractive (albeit a little futuristic) remember that we must also consider our users. The primary users for this system are intended to be elderly people living alone. We have already established (in Activity 4 of Block 2 Unit 2) that the user profile has a strong emphasis on novice users, and a sense of distrust or uncertainty surrounding the use of software technology. It therefore seems unlikely that this user group would be comfortable with a system that takes too much control of the process. If you consider an essential use case for the kind of system envisioned above, then there is very little for the user to do, and control rests largely with the technology. Given these characteristics, the most suitable paradigm is likely to be either a standard GUI desktop or a mobile device. In Computer Activity 2 we discussed the possibility of a mobile device, but found several disadvantages with this paradigm. A GUI desktop system attached to the television is likely to be more appropriate.

Having explored the problem space, and considered interaction mode, interaction paradigm and interface metaphors, you will have an outline of the conceptual model alternatives for your product. The third activity involves expanding this outline.

2.5 How to expand the conceptual model

The Set Book suggests three questions that need to be considered when expanding the conceptual model outline: what functions will the product perform, how are the functions related to each other, and what information needs to be available? We will consider each of these in turn.

2.5.1 What functions will the product perform, and what will the user do?

When the conceptual model is expanded, the designer needs to consider what exactly the product will do, and what the user will be expected to do, i.e. how will the task be divided between user and product. The example cited in the Set Book is the shared calendar and whether the system itself should book appointments automatically, or whether the user should be left with the ultimate responsibility. When we considered the interaction paradigm for KitchenMade, similar considerations were taken into account. Another example for this system is whether to insist that users must enter their dietary requirements before being able to choose recipes. Although the main purpose of the system is to provide guidance based on the user's situation, the user may want to browse recipes without this restriction. The key question is concerned with control, and whether the interactive product or the user is responsible for a decision.

I highlighted earlier the importance of questioning assumptions that may have arisen early in development, or that are built into scenarios and storyboards. One area where assumptions are often made is in relation to the division of tasks between user and product.

ACTIVITY 6

The one-stop car shop scenarios and storyboard assume that certain tasks will be performed by the user and some by the product. Identify the tasks the user will perform and those the product will perform, according to the scenario on page 226 of the Set Book. Consider this division and suggest alternatives that might be appropriate.

COMMENT

At present, the car-shop system passively provides information and runs the simulations as requested by the user. The control is left very much to the user to direct the experience, and she can choose which information to browse, when to start the simulations and when to finish the session altogether. Some users may be as organised as this, and may be sufficiently prepared to run such a session successfully. However, if you consider the role of a sales person in a car showroom, they are often called upon to make recommendations and to suggest alternatives. It would be possible for the product itself to take over some of this control. For example, the system could recommend particular cars to look at, or suggest similar vehicles to the ones already considered. These decisions would be made by considering the user profile and, ultimately by asking representative users about their preferences.

A different, but related, issue is which aspects of the interface will be controlled by software and which will be controlled by hard switches or buttons. For example, the screen for many PDAs is large enough to display a keyboard which is then 'typed' on using a stylus or fingertips. Other hand-held devices have an integrated physical keyboard. For example, Figure 15.1 on page 465 in the Set Book illustrates the Nokia 9210 communicator which has a physical keyboard integrated with the phone.

2.5.2   How are the functions related to each other?

Review Question 17

The issue of task relationship was discussed in Block 2 and again on pages 258–9 of the Set Book. What representations have already been introduced to capture task relationships?

The three main relationships between tasks that have been mentioned so far are: tasks and sub-tasks, sequencing, and categorisation. These relationships will influence how the tasks are designed into the product, e.g. by structuring screens around a task hierarchy, grouping related tasks together, and so on.

These relationships may have already been captured during the requirements activity. If so, they may be expressed using representations such as HTA diagrams, UML diagrams, and so on. Categories may have been identified using affinity diagrams. Alternatively, they could be represented as simple lists. At this stage, it is not significant to worry about which representation they appear in, provided that each task has been analysed and relationships have been identified. Remember to question your assumptions and to consider at each stage whether your understanding of the requirements and your analysis have been challenged by new information you receive as design progresses.

Taking KitchenMade as an example, there are two main sub-tasks for the system: entering the user's data and choosing a suitable recipe. These two sub-tasks are related sequentially in that if the system knows about the user's dietary requirements then it can help more effectively in choosing a recipe. They are also related because the recipe-choosing task needs to be able to make use of the user's data. For example if the user is diabetic, then the system needs to know whether a particular recipe is suitable for diabetics, or at least whether it can be modified for a diabetic diet.

2.5.3   What information needs to be available?

For each of the tasks that the product will support, we need to identify the information it requires. As mentioned in the Set Book, data requirements will have been identified during the requirements activity, but it will not have been related to specific tasks. This can be captured using a simple list. Take the tasks that need to be performed and list against each one the data that's needed. This will feed into interface design when we consider how the task is divided across screens, and what information needs to be on each screen (see Section 3 below).

For example, KitchenMade is designed to support the task of finding cheap and easy recipes. The first sub-task (entering user-specific data) requires the user's allergies, preferences, dislikes, medical requirements (such as diabetes, low-carbohydrate food), and so on. This information will be needed in order to search the set of recipes that the system holds. For the second sub-task (choosing a suitable recipe) this information will need to be available to the system so that it can choose an appropriate recipe, but it need not necessarily be shown to the user.

2.6 How to develop a card-based prototype

The Set Book introduces card-based prototypes on page 263, and you were asked to produce a card-based prototype in Activity 8.6. This kind of prototype can be used to explore the elements of the conceptual model discussed above, i.e. the division of tasks across screens, the relationship between tasks, and the information required for each task to be undertaken (what needs to be available on each screen). One card may be used to represent one view of the whole interface, or elements of that view. A card-based prototype may also be used to test out different interface metaphors and interaction modes. Remember that in Section 2.2 I said that if it is unclear as to whether the mode should be object-based or activity-based, then the designer could prototype both and evaluate them with the users.

To develop a card-based prototype, the best place to start is to step through the task that the user will perform. The scenarios and use cases developed in the requirements activity will help here, although they may have been modified as a result of earlier conceptual design stages. In Block 2 Unit 2 Activity 14 the following use case was developed for Albert's KitchenMade scenario:

1   The system presents the user with a list of options.

2   The user chooses the option to select main meals.

3   The system prompts the user to enter information about cost constraints and complexity of recipe.

4   The user types in the information.

5   The system displays a sequence of video clips.

6   The user makes a choice of one of the video clips.

7   The user chooses to print a list of ingredients for his recipe choice.

8   The system prints the list.

Alternative courses:

6   If the user does not choose any of the video clips:

   6.1 The system prompts the user to choose whether to view more clips, view certain clips again or to exit the system.

   6.2 The system returns to step 5, or exits.

7   If the user does not choose to print the list of ingredients:

   7.1 The system prints a suitable message and exits.

This use case could be translated directly into a card-based prototype. If we did this, then the first card might look like the one shown in Figure 5. This card shows a list of options for the user to choose a meal. The prototype doesn't indicate how the user can choose these, but we don't need to worry about that at the moment. Note that I have had to make some assumptions about the options to offer the user. These may or may not be appropriate, and it is only when testing with users that we'll find out.

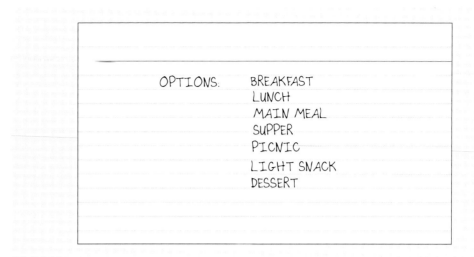

Figure 5   The first card of the card-based prototype for KitchenMade use case

ACTIVITY 7

The next use case step requires prompting for cost constraints and recipe complexity. (Note that this will be the same no matter which meal type is chosen in the first step.) Consider the main purpose of this step, i.e. to elicit information from the user about the cost and complexity of the recipe she is looking for. Think about what this element should contain, and sketch it out on a card-sized piece of paper, like the one in Figure 5. Remember that you should be focusing on the content rather than details of the layout.

COMMENT

I came up with two different sketches, which are shown in Figures 6(a) and 6(b). When it came to specifying the cost and complexity options, it became clear that we don't yet have any information about what these two criteria mean. Also, how are these criteria related to other characteristics of the meal? Do you have different cost ranges depending on which meal type has been chosen? What are the reasonable cost ranges? How do you measure 'complexity'? For example, it could refer to the number of cooking utensils used in a recipe, the number of different ingredients used, the length of preparation required, how skilled the cook needs to be (e.g. cooking Baked Alaska took me four goes before I mastered how to prevent ice cream from melting all over my oven!), and so on.

(a)

(b)

Figure 6 Further screens of the KitchenMade card-based prototype

Producing even relatively simple screen elements like those in Figure 6 has identified some questions which we would need to investigate further, either through prototyping or discussions with users.

ACTIVITY 8

The next step in the use case after the user has chosen their options is 'The system displays a sequence of video clips'. Consider the interface metaphors discussed above for choosing recipes in KitchenMade, i.e. cookery book and television. Using each one as a guide in turn, consider how the system might perform this step, i.e. think about the cookery book metaphor and produce a card sketch that would correspond to this step in the use case, then think about the television metaphor and sketch an alternative design.

COMMENT

My two sketches are shown in Figures 7(a) and 7(b). You may have come up with sketches that look quite different from mine, depending on which characteristics of the metaphors you chose to focus upon, how you interpreted the use case step, and what level of user control you felt would be appropriate. For example, if you interpreted the step literally, so that the system starts running the video clips immediately, one after the other, you would have to decide how the user could stop the show, and how to choose the recipe.

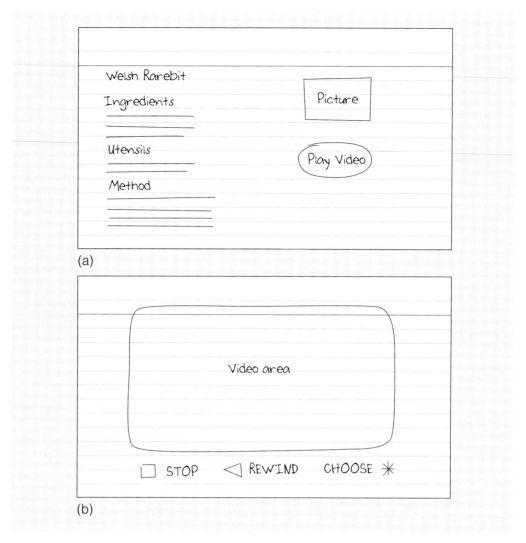

(a)

(b)

Figure 7 Different card-based prototype screens

Alternatively, when thinking about the cookery book metaphor, you may have chosen to display a 'page' (screen) per recipe from where the user can run the corresponding video. In this case, they would also be able to look through the details of the recipe.

Using the television metaphor might lead you to consider having the equivalent of different channels running different videos at the same time, where users can switch between them.

You will learn how to do evaluation more formally in Block 4.

Having explored some ideas for the conceptual model through this form of card-based prototyping, I showed my initial designs to a potential user of the system. In particular, I focused on the screens for playing a video. On this occasion, I simply showed the user the cards and explained what the system was intended to do. Of the two designs, he preferred the first layout, based on a cookery book. He said that this was familiar. He also said that he would expect to see more information on this screen, e.g. cost of the meal, how many people the quantities are for, and the cooking time. When playing the video, he would also expect the image to fill the screen so that it could be seen easily.

The user was not so keen on the second design, based on a television. His first reaction was that he wanted a remote control to operate the video buttons, and then he suggested an interaction similar to Ceefax, in which the user can switch between pages of text and images. His main concern with this interface seemed to be that the video sequence would be too fast and confusing.

As we discussed the interaction further, he suggested that a sequence of still photographs showing the major steps in the recipe might be more helpful and would allow users to go at their own pace. This idea could in fact be merged with the idea of a video, where the video automatically stops at certain stages and can be rewound to the beginning of a stage.

Producing a card-based prototype is a good starting point for thinking about design decisions and utilising the metaphors, different paradigms, interaction modes etc that have been considered during the development of the conceptual model. It is also something concrete that you can take to potential users and get informal feedback, which can then form the basis of redesign and re-thinking. For example, we did not consider either the idea of still photos or the Ceefax metaphor in our earlier design discussions.

I hope that from Activities 7 and 8, and the description of the informal feedback session, you have begun to understand how developing a card-based prototype helps you to explore the different elements of a conceptual model. But we have only just scratched the surface here. For the real system we would modify these screens in light of the feedback. They would be re-drawn, evaluated with users, modified again, and so on several times before we considered detailed interface design. Getting terminology, task flow, support features (such as help), interaction mode, and metaphor right are important design decisions which can be tested out using cards. Some of the issues are illustrated in Computer Activity 3.

ACTIVITY

Computer Activity 3: Extending and reviewing a card-based prototype
This activity will take approximately 45 minutes.

This computer activity illustrates how the card-based prototype for KitchenMade may be extended and then reviewed with a user.

3 Physical design: getting concrete

3.1 Review of the Set Book reading

This section of the Set Book looks briefly at **physical design**, i.e. at producing detailed designs of the interface for the interactive product. As part of the iterative nature of interaction design, the process will cycle between conceptual design and physical design (and indeed back to the requirements activity). There is therefore no set boundary between these two inter-related activities.

You met a variety of guidelines and standards in Blocks 1 and 2. Section 8.4 of the Set Book provides an overview of the different kinds of guidance available.

The Set Book discusses menu design, icon design, screen design, information display and design guidelines and standards. It introduces Shneiderman's eight golden rules of interface design, which extend the design principles you met in Block 1 of visibility, feedback, constraints, mapping, consistency and affordance. There are many other aspects of physical design such as use of colour, device design (e.g. for mobile phones, remote control units, wearable computers), toolbar behaviour, help systems, and so on. This course will not be covering all of these, as detailed product design would justify a course in itself!

Review Question 18

Design is about balancing requirements which are often in conflict. What kind of conflict in requirements might be evident for the physical design of a video game?

Review Question 19

What is the relationship between design guidelines and the work of cognitive science introduced in Unit 3 of this block?

Review Question 20

Consistency is one of the golden rules listed on page 266 of the Set Book. But there are times when a designer might choose to be inconsistent deliberately. Under what circumstances might inconsistency be chosen?

Review Question 21

List four characteristics of a good icon, and state two heuristics for good icon design.

ACTIVITY 9

Consider a website that you use regularly. Apply the eight golden rules introduced on page 266 of the Set Book to the site. How many rules does it obey? Can you find any examples where the rules are broken? What effect does this have on your interaction with the site?

COMMENT

I use the Amazon book store often (http://www.amazon.co.uk), and so base my assessment on this site.

Strive for consistency. The pages of the site generally have the same structure and same look and feel. For example, the menus across the top and sides are consistently present. The information available for each book is the same, and its presentation is consistent. I could not find any inconsistencies here.

Enable frequent users to use shortcuts. Interestingly, this site provides short cuts specifically tailored for me. It recommends books that I might want to buy, based on my previous purchases. There is a 'one-click' option which remembers who I am and my payments and delivery details, which is another example of supporting frequent users of the site.

Offer informative feedback. When it can't find a book I'm looking for, it politely tells me so, and suggests results for the closest thing it can find. For example, if I search for author Yiddell it says that it can't find Yiddell but can find Waddell. You may well argue that this is not exactly helpful, but it may be that I mis-typed the name, or it may be that I will find equally interesting books by this other author.

Design dialogues to yield closure. When I buy a book, it says clearly that my order has been placed.

Offer error prevention and simple error handling. The site makes it quite difficult to make errors, but if, for example, I purchase a book and then need to cancel it, I can amend my order.

Permit easy reversal of actions. If I place a book in my basket and then decide I don't want it, I can remove it with a single click.

Support internal locus of control. I am asked for confirmation before anything significant happens. I feel in complete control.

Reduce short-term memory load. This site is very good at this, and carries forward my details from one screen to the next.

This website is quite mature and refined, so it is not surprising that it meets all of the golden rules. Maybe your site did not?

There are many sets of guidelines for designing interactive products, specifically geared for different application domains. In this section we will explore two areas further: one related to accessibility in interaction and one intended to cater for cultural issues (as introduced in Block 2 Unit 1). I will then explain how to develop the third and most detailed kind of prototype that we shall be introducing in this course: interface sketches.

3.2 Universal usability

The Universal Usability movement believes that design should cater for a wide range of needs and abilities. Therefore a design should be flexible and enable alternative methods of interaction.

Block 2 Unit 1, and Unit 2 in this block, discussed some of the issues around designing for accessibility. Here I provide some more detail on what this means by introducing some guidelines and principles for universal access. The emphasis is not only to enable the disabled, but also to make the use of systems easier for all users.

Ron Mace, from the Center for Universal Design at North Carolina State University, defines universal design as:

> Universal design is the design of products and environments to be usable by all people, to the greatest extent possible, without the need for adaptation or specialized design.

To this end, the Center has developed seven principles of universal design to support accessibility. They are listed in Table 2.

Table 3   The principles of universal design

Principle	Description
Equitable use	The design is useful and marketable to people with diverse abilities.
Flexibility in use	The design accommodates a wide range of individual preferences and abilities.
Simple and intuitive* use	Use of the design is easy to understand, regardless of the user's experience, knowledge, language skills, or current concentration level.
Perceptible information	The design communicates necessary information effectively to the user, regardless of ambient conditions or the user's sensory abilities.
Tolerance for error	The design minimises hazards and the adverse consequences of accidental or unintended actions.
Low physical effort	The design can be used efficiently and comfortably with a minimum of fatigue.
Size and space for approach and use	Appropriate size and space is provided for approach, reach, manipulation, and use regardless of user's body size, posture, or mobility.

* The term 'intuitive' is rather ambiguous – what's intuitive to me won't necessarily be intuitive to you. It is a term that is avoided in many interaction design circles.

Source: http://www.design.ncsu.edu:8120/cud/univ_design/poster.pdf

These guidelines are not intended specifically for software-based interactive products but also include doorways, handles and knobs, ticket barriers, and so on. There are however some comparisons to be made between this list and the set of design implications presented in Unit 3, and Chapter 3 pages 77–89 of the Set Book. For example, one of the design implications for reading is to make opportunities available to

enlarge the text, which leads to a flexible system; providing additional hidden information (an implication from decision-making) also leads to equitable use and flexibility.

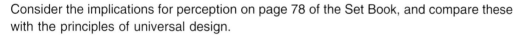

ACTIVITY 10

Consider the implications for perception on page 78 of the Set Book, and compare these with the principles of universal design.

COMMENT

These implications touch on several of the principles, and in particular expands on the principle 'perceptible information'.

3.3 | Designing for cultural diversity

You learned in Block 2 about the different cultural dimensions suggested by Hofstede, and about how these dimensions have been interpreted by interaction designers. There, you were introduced to a set of questions that interaction designers should consider before starting design, so that the user's culture is taken into account. These questions are:

1 What will motivate users?

2 How much conflict can people tolerate in content or style of argumentation?

3 What role exists for personal opinion as opposed to group opinion?

4 What is valued more, lack of ambiguity or potential for exploration?

5 How much advertising hyperbole is expected (or can be tolerated)?

6 Should an online help system act like a guru with the definitive answer, or a friend suggesting possibilities?

Considering these questions helps you to understand the potential users of the product, will shape the user profile that you construct, and then the user profile informs design.

However, these questions are useful only when you are designing for a particular culture. If you are designing for an international audience, then these questions are less helpful. One way to design for an international audience is to identify aspects of the product that will need to be culture-specific, and those that will not. Then design suitable alternatives for those culture-specific aspects you have identified. Another approach is to design the product to be as international as possible.

The following guidelines, taken from Esselink (2000), are intended to help international design.

1   Be careful about using images that depict hand gestures or people.

2   Use generic icons.

3   Choose colours that are not associated with national flags or political movements.

4   Ensure that the product supports different calendars, date formats, and time formats.

5   Ensure that the product supports different number formats, currencies, weights and measurement systems.

6   Ensure that the product supports international paper sizes, envelope sizes and address formats.

7   Avoid integrating text in graphics as they cannot be translated easily.

8   Allow for text expansion when translated from English.

These are a mixture of design principles and design rules (as discussed in Box 8.5 of the Set Book) because some are abstract and require interpretation while others are more specific.

ACTIVITY 11

The user profile for potential KitchenMade users (from Block 2 Unit 2, Activity 4) identified some cultural values:

> Users may have strong uncertainty avoidance and feel more comfortable with strongly structured tasks which provide detailed guidance on how to proceed. The implications for requirements are that tasks should be clearly structured; the system should convey the reassurance that it has been developed with nutrition experts, and the design elements should appeal to older users.

How might you take this into account in designing the system? If this was being designed for an international audience, what features would you include?

COMMENT

The structure for tasks could be provided by clear and careful step-by-step recipe instructions. We have already discussed that these could be communicated using video, or written instructions. Conveying that the recipes have been developed by experts could be achieved by having an introduction by the chefs, dieticians and others who have contributed recipes, and by having a clear explanation of why this particular recipe is suitable for the user.

If KitchenMade was being developed for an international audience, then the guidelines above for international design would need to be taken into account. Apart from translation, the basic design of the system could be the same except for the videos. They would need to be recorded with people native to the target culture doing the cooking and explaining the recipe. The product would also need to take into account different measurements systems and formats. It is also likely that the recipes themselves would need to be tailored for local produce and preferences.

3.4 How to develop an interface sketch

Section 8.4 of the Set Book discusses several elements of physical design: menu design, icon design, screen design and information display. Screen design involves two elements: how the task is split across screens and the detail of the screen design itself. Card-based prototypes can be used to prototype and evaluate the former, i.e. how the task is split, but they are not suitable for evaluating any other elements of physical design in any depth. To do this requires a more detailed interface design. It is possible to build up a very detailed paper-based prototype that can be 'run' by a person pretending to be the computer, and involving masking tape, acetate sheets, and various other paper products. This is described further in Snyder (2003, p. 259) if you are interested in pursuing this at a later date. However, in this course you will be asked only to sketch detailed screens and other interface elements. These can be used to step through tasks with a user, and to consider aspects of detailed design, but they are not intended to be complex.

Evaluation of interactive products will be addressed in Block 4.

There are different places to start when developing a sketch of the interface. As this is readily available, I suggest that you use a complete A4 sheet of paper to represent your interface. If the application is to run on a desktop, then this sheet of paper will represent the whole screen, but if you are designing a hand-held device then the sheet may represent the whole interface. In this case, the screen size may be tightly limited and you need to make sure that your design fits comfortably within the limits. Computer Activity 4 will introduce you to some issues related to mobile phone design.

An interface sketch would normally be developed after a card-based prototype has been produced, and some feedback elicited from potential users of the system. This feedback can be used to progress the interface design as described below. Remember that development is iterative and that these decisions will be revisited after further development and evaluation.

1   Was the task split identified in your card-based prototype appropriate, or does this need to be changed? If so, how?

2   Does your application need to be consistent with other applications? If so, then you need to identify these elements first, especially if they influence interface layout. For example, if the application is to run under the Windows operating system, then the application needs to comply with the Windows style guide. Among other things, this comments on the use of menus and the style of help to offer. Sketch these onto your piece of paper first so that these constraints will be clearly accounted for.

3   What elements need to be included in the interface you are sketching? You will have made some decisions about this when developing the card-based prototype. Review this and any feedback you have received about it.

4   Which elements of the interface do you want users' attention to be drawn to when they first arrive at this point? How will this be achieved? How will you design the interface in order to ensure that users are not distracted?

5   What mechanisms will the users need to indicate control such as choosing options or choosing the next stage of the task? This might include menus, buttons, shortcut keys, etc. If using menus, what will they be used for? How will they be organised and accessed? If using buttons, what should they look like (e.g. size) and what will they do? You might want to use drop-down lists for choosing options, check boxes or radio buttons (see examples of these in Figure 8). Radio buttons allow only one option to be chosen. Check-list boxes allow several (all) boxes to be checked. Drop-down lists offer options to the user when the arrow button is clicked on.

6   Does this interface require icons, or would the interface be enhanced by using icons (e.g. by replacing a large amount of text with a small icon)? If so, what icons are

needed? Are there commonly-available icons that could be used here, or do you need to design your own?

7   Are there clear groupings of information or commands that will make the interface easier to use? If so, how will you represent this grouping? By colour, space, borders, etc?

8   What kind of information needs to be displayed? How can this best be represented?

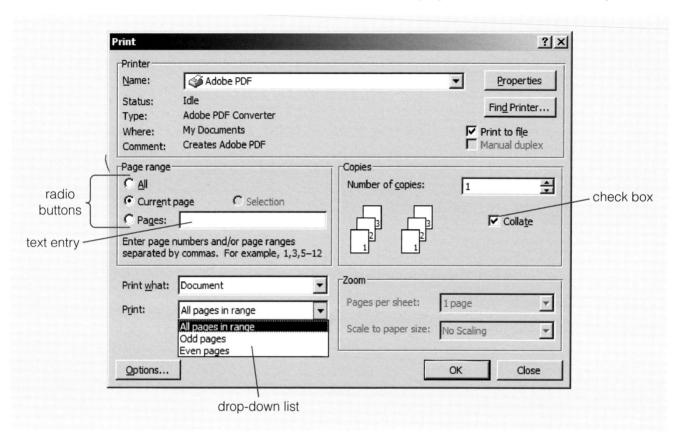

Figure 8   The Windows print dialogue box showing examples of radio buttons, check boxes, drop-down lists and text entry

As we discussed in Section 2.6 above, the potential user has given us some feedback on the initial card-based prototype for KitchenMade. He said that he preferred the cookery book interface to the television interface, but that he would also like to see a full-screen video. We also have some feedback from the user we saw in Computer Activity 3. I have therefore decided to develop both of these alternatives in more detail, perhaps with the idea of combining them, but for now I will concentrate on producing an interface sketch for the cookery-book interface. To do this, consider each of the questions listed above:

1   *Task split.* The user liked the cookery book page but wanted more detailed information about the recipe and also to have the video fill the whole screen. The task split seems to be suitable provided the screen doesn't get too cluttered.

2   *Consistency with other applications.* From the user profile we know that the users of this system are novice computer users. Consistency with other software packages is therefore unlikely to be important. I shall assume that there are no requirements for consistency with other systems.

3   *What elements need to be included in the interface?* The interface needs to include details of the recipe: name, ingredients list, utensils list, complexity, cost, number of people, method steps, and a picture of the dish. In addition, the user profile suggests that users want to know that the recipes have been developed by nutrition experts, so it may be a good idea to include the name of the person who

recommended this recipe. It may also be useful to include the user's name, meal selected, date and time. These suggestions are based on considering the user profile, user experience goals and usability goals, as identified in Activity 4 of Block 2 Unit 2.

4   *Which elements should the user's attention be drawn to?* If we have a picture of the meal, then the users' attention will be drawn there. It will be important to find a suitable photograph of the meal so that it is clear, inviting and cheerful. Other places to draw to the user's attention are: the cost and complexity of the recipe chosen, the meal for which the recommendation is made, the name of the dish, and the person who recommended the recipe.

5   *What mechanisms of control are needed?* For this screen, the main control items would need to be to play the video, print the ingredients and leave this recipe page. The controls should be simple. Perhaps one button to play the video, one button to choose a different recipe, one button to print the ingredients and one button to leave the system.

6   *Does this interface require icons?* At this stage it is unclear what icons would be appropriate, if any. It does not seem suitable to have an icon to play the video or to signify text elements, but this decision can be revisited later. You could have icons to represent the time, etc., similar to those used in this course to represent Set Book, use of internet, etc.

7   *Are there clear groupings of information?* There are some clear groupings, e.g. of parts of the recipe such as ingredients, steps in the method, etc. These could be grouped by colour, by border or by physical proximity.

8   *What kind of information needs to be displayed?* The information here is mostly text, so this is how it should be represented. If the recipe were to have some information about grammes of salt, or fat index, then this information might be shown graphically with a scale of some kind.

Having considered all of the above, I produced the interface sketch shown in Figure 9 overleaf. Note that I did not produce this sketch straight away. It is the result of several iterations of sketching, rubbing out, modifying, re-sketching and so on. And even so, there is still much that can be improved in it.

You'll see that the areas for highlighting have been coloured differently from the background, and I have also used different techniques for grouping related items: the recipe sections are on the left and have been grouped using one line colour, while the control buttons are on the right and have been grouped using a different line style. The use of colour in the interface is beyond the scope of this course, but using different styles to group similar elements on the screen is a useful technique. Also, Albert's name and the choice of meal are displayed at the top of the screen, together with some other elements. This is now ready to be evaluated more formally by potential users, but before doing that it would be helpful to have the video screen developed to the same level of detail.

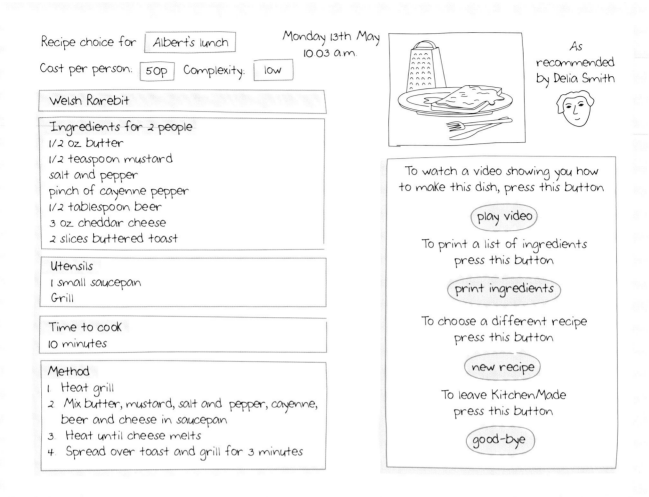

Figure 9   An initial sketch for the cookery book interface to KitchenMade

ACTIVITY 12

Consider the video screen for KitchenMade which was shown in Figure 7(b). Step through the list of questions above and produce an interface sketch for it. You should assume that the intention is to combine this alternative with the cookery book, so that this screen controls the playing of the video. You may find it helpful to refer to Activity 4 in Block 2 Unit 2 where a set of requirements was developed.

COMMENT

My sketch is shown in Figure 10 overleaf. You may have answered the questions below in a different way and hence produced a different sketch. This is fine provided that your decisions are informed by the requirements including the user profile, usability goals and user experience goals. The main part of this design was to look at the control mechanisms and how the user would interact with them.

1   *Task split.* The user has suggested that the video should take up the whole of the screen, so there is no other split to consider.

2   *Consistency with other applications.* I decided above that there did not need to be any consistency with other software but the interface should be true to the television metaphor on which it is based, in order to preserve familiarity.

3   *What elements need to be included in the interface?* The main element of the interface is the video playing area. Other elements required are control buttons for the video and for leaving this screen. In addition, some of the details at the top of the cookery book screen may be helpful to remind the user of the recipe and the meal being prepared.

4   *Which elements should the user's attention be drawn to?* The main area for attention is the video playing area, although users should be able to find the control buttons easily as well.

5   *What mechanisms of control are needed?* Standard controls for the video would be stop, play, fast forward, and rewind. Given the task and the users, I would also include pause and a control to step through the sequence frame-by-frame so that the user can follow the steps more slowly. I chose to use an icon to represent this step function.

6   *Does this interface require icons?* There are standard icons for all the video controls except the frame-by-frame step function.

7   *Are there clear groupings of information?* The control buttons need to be positioned together, but carefully so that the user is unlikely to choose to leave the system accidentally.

8   *What kind of information needs to be displayed?* Only video and control information are needed.

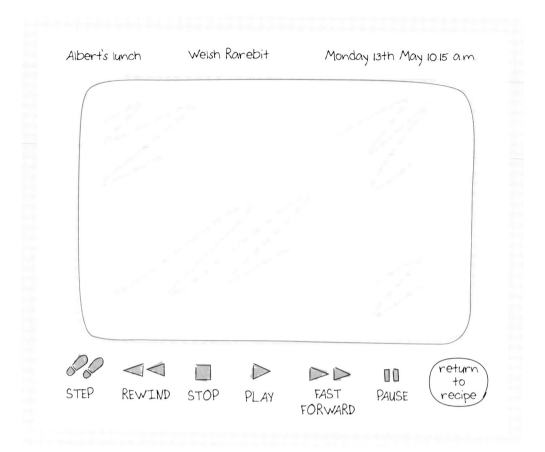

Figure 10   An initial sketch for the television interface to KitchenMade

---

Review Question 22

Suggest suitable interaction devices for KitchenMade

In the KitchenMade example, the interface was mainly concerned with software, however other devices will require an interface that includes physical design as well as software design. The following computer activity involves the design of a physical interface.

ACTIVITY

Computer Activity 4: Designing a mobile phone

This activity will take approximately one hour.

This computer activity asks you to design mobile phones for two different characters. It will give you the opportunity to explore interface design for a familiar interactive device, and to experience some of the design trade-offs that need to be made for different user groups.

Before performing this activity, I suggest that you read Box 15.1 on page 470 of the Set Book. This introduces some of the design questions related to interfaces for mobile devices.

4 Tool support

4.1 Review of the Set Book reading

> **STUDY NOTE**
>
> This section complements and extends Section 8.5 in the Set Book. If you have not already read Section 8.5 of the Set Book, then I suggest that you do so before reading any further.

Tools to support interaction design come in a variety of types. There are also new tools being developed all the time – technology moves faster than our ability to write about it. Hence, this section focuses on some general comments about interface design tools. You will get the chance to experience a more modern tool through the computer activity below.

Review Question 23

One of the facilities suggested for user interface software tools is that it might help the user to 'create easy-to-use interfaces' (page 275 of the Set Book). Briefly describe how a software tool might be able to achieve this.

ACTIVITY

Computer Activity 5: A tool to support low-fidelity prototyping

This activity will take approximately 45 minutes.

In this activity, you will see a video of a tool to support the early design of websites.

5 Summary of Unit 4

This unit has introduced you to a variety of different techniques for developing and prototyping a conceptual model for an interactive product. This unit is rather long because it pulls together the material presented in Block 2 and Units 1 to 3 of this block. The information you gleaned from these earlier units supports and informs the development of the conceptual model and the prototypes derived from it.

The conceptual model is informed and guided by many things:

▶ the product's requirements

▶ the user profile of potential users of the product

▶ cognitive considerations applicable to all human beings

▶ different paradigms that exist

▶ other sources of inspiration.

Keeping these issues in mind all the time is a demanding task, which is why I have stressed the need to question assumptions, to iterate, and to get feedback from potential users.

The three activities involved in producing a conceptual model are:

1   Explore the problem space of the intended product.

2   Consider different aspects of the conceptual model: interaction mode, interface metaphor and interaction paradigm.

3   Flesh out the outline conceptual model by considering what functions will the product perform and what will the user perform, how are these functions related, and what information needs to be available for these functions.

More detailed design also needs to take these issues into consideration and there are many sets of design principles and rules to help. Some of these are very general and are therefore difficult to apply effectively; others are more specific. In this unit, I have only dealt with a sub-set of the issues concerned with detailed physical design. For example, I have not discussed the use of colour, or different typefaces at all, and I have only looked briefly at grouping mechanisms, information display and dialogue design. The physical design of interfaces would justify a course in itself!

The three different kinds of prototype you have met and developed in this unit can each help assess different aspects of the design under development. Figure 11 below is a copy of Figure 1 that I presented in the Introduction to Unit 4. I have repeated it here to emphasise the different prototypes and their strengths.

Each of the activities mentioned above will be iterated and assessed as the design is refined. Once sufficient detail has been sorted out and evaluated, the next step would be to begin higher-fidelity prototyping, and then building the final product.

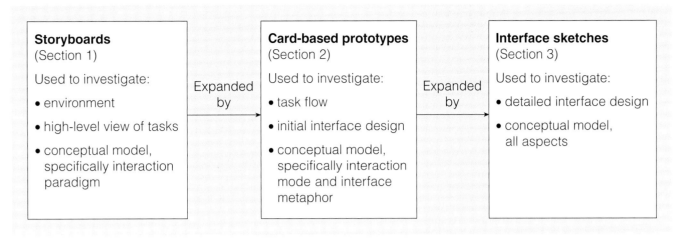

Figure 11   The three different prototypes introduced in this unit, and how they relate

References

Esselink, B. (2000) *A Practical Guide to Localisation*, Amsterdam, John Benjamins Publishing Company.

Mayhew, D.J. (1999) *The Usability Engineering Lifecycle*, Morgan Kaufmann.

Snyder, C. (2003) *Paper Prototyping*, Morgan Kaufmann.

Unit learning outcomes

Having studied this unit, you should be able to:

LO19: Describe prototyping and different types of prototyping activities. If you are unsure about this then look again at Review Questions 1 to 7.

LO20: Explain the benefits of paper-based prototyping. If you are unsure about this then take another look at the experience described in Box 1.

LO21: Develop and expand a conceptual model for an interactive product. This involves choosing an appropriate interaction mode and interaction paradigm, identifying and assessing alternative interface metaphors and expanding these ideas as described in Section 8.3.2 of the Set Book. If you are unsure about this then you should look again at Sections 2.2 to 2.5 of this unit.

LO22: Develop three kinds of low-fidelity prototype for an interactive product: a storyboard, a card-based prototype, and a detailed interface sketch. If you are unsure about this then you should look at Activities 1, 7 and 12, and Computer Activities 1, 2 and 3.

LO23: Apply a suitable set of design principles and rules for the design of an interactive product. If you are still unsure about this then take a look at Activities 8 and 10.

LO24: Design an appropriate icon for use in a low-fidelity prototype. If you are unsure about this then take a look at pages 270–271 including Activity 8.7 in the Set Book.

These contribute to the course learning outcomes as illustrated below.

Linking the unit learning outcomes to the course learning outcomes

Unit learning outcomes	Course learning outcomes
LO19	KU2: Define key terms in interaction design KS2: Communicate effectively to peers and specialists about requirements, design, and evaluation activities relating to interactive products.
LO19 and LO20	KU5: Explain the importance of iteration, evaluation and prototyping in interaction design KS1: Construct and convey an argument from a variety of sources to persuade a non-specialist audience of the importance of user-centred design when designing interactive products
LO21, LO22, LO23 and LO24	CS4: Produce a low-fidelity prototype for an interactive product based upon a simple list of interaction design principles

Comments on review questions

REVIEW QUESTION 1 ....

A prototype allows users to interact with an envisioned product, to gain some experiences of using it in a realistic setting, and to explore imagined uses (page 241 in the Set Book).

REVIEW QUESTION 2 ....

Low-fidelity prototypes exhibit no automatic interaction and are built using materials unlike those of the final product. They are intended for exploration only. A high-fidelity prototype exhibits some automatic interaction and is built using materials close to the final product.

(a) For this purpose, a high-fidelity prototype would be needed so that network connections can be tested.

(b) For this kind of purpose, a low-fidelity prototype would be sufficient.

REVIEW QUESTION 3 ....

Low-fidelity prototypes are used early in development because they are quick, simple and cheap to produce and to modify, and are therefore ideal for exploring ideas (page 243 of the Set Book).

REVIEW QUESTION 4 ....

There are several possible answers to this, and you may have thought of different reasons. However, one of the key characteristics of low-fidelity prototypes is that they are quick and easy to change. When designing screen layout, it can be very important to have this capability otherwise the process necessary to change a screen, or to explore alternative layouts, may be long and involved, and therefore would discourage such changes from being made. In addition, with a sketched interface it may be possible to change the layout quickly within the current session, i.e. while the user is still present, so that ideas can be checked quickly and modified again if necessary.

REVIEW QUESTION 5 ....

Yes, there is no restriction on the kind of prototype for horizontal or vertical treatment.

REVIEW QUESTION 6 ....

Evolutionary prototyping involves iteratively evolving the prototype into the final product.

Throw-away prototyping involves producing many prototypes that are intended to be thrown away.

In the former case, the quality assurance and testing regime must be commensurate with the intention that it will become the final product. In the latter case such rigorous testing is not needed, but it is important to resist any temptation to build the final product using these prototypes.

REVIEW QUESTION 7 ....

The kind of storyboard depicted in Figure 8.2 (page 243) and Figure 8.4 (page 245) of the Set Book are useful when it is helpful to portray a series of physical actions, and to capture the environment within which the product will be used. If the task involves only screen shots of a system or product, for example, then this kind of storyboarding is not so helpful. Using index cards to sketch screen shots is a more appropriate approach under these circumstances (as discussed on page 244 and as illustrated on page 263 of the Set Book).

REVIEW QUESTION 8 ....

Finding problems with requirements and functionality would probably have more impact on the redesign than the other issues, although issues with the work flow and information display could be equally influential. The other issues listed here may not cause a great impact on the redesign from the developer's point of view, but they will be very significant for the users. If terminology is wrong or confusing, then the system will be unusable.

REVIEW QUESTION 9 ....

The users matched the profile of a typical user and the tasks were realistic. These two aspects are very important if your usability testing is to be beneficial.

REVIEW QUESTION 10 ....

One design decision is that the system will need to print a shopping list for Albert to be able to take the list shopping with him. This implies that the system is not portable. The person who wrote this scenario may therefore be assuming that the system is running on a desktop PC or something similar. The scenario also talks about playing video clips, which similarly has implications for design such as the choice of output device, i.e. a high-resolution screen.

REVIEW QUESTION 11 ....

Sketching storyboards forces you to think about some of the detail of the interaction, e.g. in this case what is the environment like, what equipment should be available and how should it be laid out. Keeping the right balance between detail and abstraction is difficult, but again is all part of the iterative nature of development. At conceptual design stage it is important to be constantly asking questions of your product, your design, and your assumptions.

REVIEW QUESTION 12 ....

Sharing experiences with a user is one of the most effective ways of understanding their perspective, even when the experience is artificial, such as in the defibrillator example. Although it does not guarantee that the designer will focus more on the user, it does mean that the designer will be able to be more empathetic with the users.

REVIEW QUESTION 13 ....

Conceptual models based on objects are used when the main product of an application is the driving force behind design; an activity-focused model is appropriate when no primary products are identified.

(a) This would result in a model based on activities. Although there will be records generated by this activity, and a letter or complaint ticket may be generated, the primary aim is to support the process.

(b) This would require a model based on objects as the main purpose is to produce the collection ticket. This might involve various activities such as taking payment, collecting user information, checking stock etc., but the primary purpose of the system is to produce the ticket.

REVIEW QUESTION 14 ....

They help because they prompt you to explore the problem space, and to understand the limits and exceptions in the situation you are designing for. How disastrous would it be if things went wrong? What's the worst that can happen? What's the most beneficial outcome?

REVIEW QUESTION 15 ....

Scenarios can support cross-discipline discussion because they are informal stories, and people are good at understanding and telling stories. One potential pitfall is the use of terminology that is then misunderstood. Storyboards, in conjunction with scenarios, can help communication and hence clarify any misunderstandings.

REVIEW QUESTION 16 ....

The conceptual model is based on an object, i.e. a worksheet. A completed worksheet is a clear, identifiable work product that is individual to a user.

REVIEW QUESTION 17 ....

Hierarchical task analysis will provide some information about how the tasks are broken down into sub-tasks. Use cases and essential use cases will represent something of the sequencing of the tasks, although they may also include assumptions that need to be challenged.

REVIEW QUESTION 18 ....

The kind of conflict here might be that the game needs to be challenging, but at the same time it must be possible for the target user group to progress through the levels, otherwise no one will want to buy it.

REVIEW QUESTION 19 ....

Guidelines are often derived from theory. For example, the first design implication on page 83 for Memory leads to the golden rule 'Reduce short-term memory load'; the second design implication for Learning, on page 87, supports the golden rule 'Offer error prevention and simple error handling'.

REVIEW QUESTION 20 ....

Inconsistency might be chosen over consistency in order to highlight something for the users' attention.

REVIEW QUESTION 21 ....

Icons should be immediately recognisable, small, simple, and culturally-independent. To create them designers should draw on existing traditions or standards, and remember that concrete objects are easier to represent than actions. These are all on page 270 of the Set Book.

REVIEW QUESTION 22 ....

The environment will be messy and sticky. The user will be doing more than one task at a time. Both input and output need to be robust. The likeliest option would be a touch-screen with sound output to read the recipes.

REVIEW QUESTION 23 ....

There are many design guidelines available which could be incorporated into a design environment. It may be possible to automatically check against these guidelines as the design evolves, or they may be used to prompt the designer.

Conclusions to Block 3

Block conclusions

This block has covered a wide variety of material focused on the activities of (re)design and prototyping and construction. In many ways, having a whole block on design without involving any evaluation is rather artificial. In a real project these activities would intertwine, with some design, some evaluation, some clarifying of requirements, and back again. One important point to remember is that design in practice is never as complicated as talking or writing about design.

Having completed this block, you should now feel confident to develop and prototype the conceptual model for an interactive product. You should also know how to produce three different kinds of prototype depending on the issues that you want to investigate.

I have mentioned assessing prototypes and getting informal feedback several times in this block. The next block will explore how to evaluate the designs you built in this block more formally.

In terms of the model of interaction design introduced in the Set Book (Figure 6.7) and reproduced below, this block has been concerned with '(re)design' and 'build an interactive version'. Block 4 focuses on 'evaluation'.

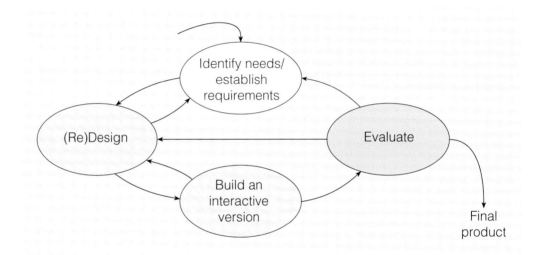

I began this block with some comments from Kees Dorst about the different approaches to design that people take. Having spent the last few weeks or so studying this block on design, I'd like to end with another extract which summarises how *not* to do design:

OK, how do you fail as a designer? Well...

Always cling to your first idea.

Jump into the details immediately.

Solve one aspect of the problem first.

Ignore a stakeholder, preferably a vital one.

First design the form, then sort out how the thing should work.

Promise too much to the client, really inflate his expectations.

Don't listen to your client, lie to him if necessary.

Be inflexible in your ideas and approach.

Try to surprise your client with a completed design.

Ignore any tests that say the design might be below par.

Wait for inspiration.

Stay 'fresh' by not gathering information.

Do not plan (because that takes too much time).

Source: Dorst, K. (2003) *Understanding Design*, BIS Publishers.

Acknowledgements

Grateful acknowledgement is made to the following sources for permission to reproduce material within this course book.

Figures

Unit 2 Figure 4: Keytools Ltd;

Unit 2 Figure 5: Keytools Ltd;

Unit 2 Figure 6: Infogrip, Inc.;

Unit 2 Figure 7: Keytools Ltd;

Unit 2 Figure 8: Palm®;

Unit 2 Figure 9: Reproduced by permission of Subzero Promotions;

Unit 2 Figure 10: Keytools Ltd;

Unit 2 Figure 11: Keytools Ltd;

Unit 2 Figure 15: Courtesy of Computer Ware;

Unit 2 Figure 16: Baber, C. (1997) Beyond the Desktop – Designing and Using Interaction Devices, Academic Press, London;

Unit 2 Figure 17(a): SensoMotoric Instruments, GmbH;

Unit 2 Figure 17(b): Tobii Technology, Sweden;

Unit 2 Figure 18: Copyright © Sony Computer Entertainment;

Unit 2 Figure 19: Iridian Technologies, Inc.;

Unit 2 Figure 20: www.palmone.com;

Unit 2 Figure 22: Copyright © Thales. Reproduced by permission;

Unit 2 Figure 23: Copyright © Paul Forster;

Unit 2 cartoon on p.40: Knight Features. Reproduced by permission;

Unit 2 cartoon on p.125: Petre, M. (1989) *Finding a Basis for Matching Programming Languages to Programming Tasks*, PhD dissertation, University College London;

Unit 3 Figure 1: Copyright © Guardian Newspapers Ltd 2004;

Unit 3 Figure 2: Copyright © Guardian Newspapers Ltd 2004;

Unit 3 Figure 3: Copyright © Guardian Newspapers Ltd 2004;

Unit 3 Figure 4: Copyright © Apple.

Text

Unit 1 Box 2: 'Wearable computing', taken from www.media.mit.edu/wearables/lizzy/mit-ideo/index.html;

Unit 4 Box 1: 'Using paper prototypes to manage risk', taken from www.uie.com/articles/prototyping_risk. Copyright © 1997–2005 User Interface Engineering

Unit 4 Table 3: taken from www.design.ncsu.edu.

Every effort has been made to contact copyright holders. If any have been inadvertently overlooked the publishers will be pleased to make the necessary arrangements at the first opportunity.